John Bailey's
Complete Guide to
FLY FISHING

John Bailey's
Complete Guide to
FLY FISHING
The Fish, the Tackle & the Techniques

CRE▲TIVE
OUTDOORS™

First published in the United States and Canada in 2004 by

CREATIVE
OUTDOORS™

An imprint of Creative Homeowner®
Upper Saddle River, NJ
Creative Homeowner® is a registered trademark of Federal Marketing Corp.

Current printing (last digit): 10 9 8 7 6 5 4 3 2
Library of Congress card number: 2004113170
ISBN 1-58011-233-1

Publishing Manager: Jo Hemmings
Senior Editor: Kate Michell
Assistant Editor: Rose Hudson
Design & Cover Design: Andrew Easton
Editor: Ian Whitelaw
Indexer: Dorothy Frame
Production: Lucy Hulme

Originated in Singapore
Printed and bound in Singapore

CREATIVE HOMEOWNER
A division of Federal Marketing Corp.
24 Park Way
Upper Saddle River
NJ 07458
www.creativehomeowner.com

CONTENTS

INTRODUCTION

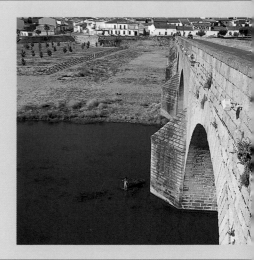

I DON'T THINK THAT THE FLY FISHERMAN HAS EVER HAD IT SO GOOD. THERE WAS A TIME, NOT LONG AGO, WHEN A SALMON ROD WEIGHED THE BEST PART OF TWO POUNDS, AND EVEN THE LIGHTER TROUT GEAR WAS A TORMENT TO USE. THIS WAS NOT ONLY PHYSICALLY CRIPPLING, BUT ALSO SPIRITUALLY DAMAGING, FOR FLY FISHING IS ALL ABOUT GRACE. IT'S A SPORT OF WHISPERING LINES, OF FEATHER-LIGHT CASTS.

The Finest of Sports

To put it simply, fly fishing is beautiful: that's why at any game fair you'll find non-anglers watching fly-casting exhibitions with total joy and amazement. Fly fishing is lovely to watch and it's lovely to execute. Think of baseball and a perfectly timed home run. Think of the delicately curving free kick as the soccer ball hits the back of the net like an exploding shell, or the perfectly executed golf swing that sends a ball seemingly eternally down the fairway, an athlete rippling cheetah-like over the hurdles, the blur of the cricket bat, or a perfect half volley over the tennis net, down the sideline and away. Fly fishing is all of these things, and the acts of snaking out a 40-yard Spey cast or flicking a light, tight line under the grabbing fingers of an overhanging tree are real physical joys that you can savor. You don't even need to see a fish to have a wonderful day with a fly rod in your hand— but when you do…

Dreams and Memories

When I was a child, fishing was the source of all my dreams, dreams that I've been privileged to live out as an adult. I can cast my mind back to countless moments of head-spinning delight—and soul-wrenching disappointment—that fly fishing has brought me…

It was in June 1963, that the neb of a great trout engulfed my little blue-winged olive the very instant it settled on the choppy waters of the lake. I'd never, ever known a fight like it. My knees, trembling between my boots and my short trousers, nearly gave out under me, and when the beaten fish went rigid over my pathetically inadequate landing net and finally broke free, I sobbed. The memory still brings tears to my eyes.

It's 1964, I'm beside a flooded Welsh river with salmon everywhere on the move, and a fish porpoises over my fly. Next cast, it takes, and the fly line slides mysteriously off into the muddied water. My first salmon is suddenly cartwheeling, cascading out of the pool and down the rapids, with me in pell-mell pursuit, shouting—no, shrieking—for help. Finally, I have him cornered in a tiny rock pool and I cradle him out—I've caught my first salmon, at last.

Steelhead in the snow; bonefish in the baking heat; grayling on a Scottish river when the air is so cold your line freezes in the rings and the spent salmon are dropping back past you, struggling their desperate way to the sea; the mayfly hatch; a sea-trout river at night; the rivers of Kashmir; the lakes of New Zealand—the memories this sport can bring us are endless.

Blessed Guardians

Fly fishing is also, without doubt, the most riveting way to explore and understand the environment. Blending into the waterside, we experience scenes, sights, and sounds that most people never will: the kingfishers piping up and down the river; the hunched-up heron in the margins; the cluck of the water hen; the stately white dagger throat of the grebe; the spiraling mayflies, gossamer wings illuminated by the gold of the sunset; the misty valley when the salmon are as steely as the

> ➤ THE TIGHTEST OF SPOTS
Tiny, overgrown streams like this call for either a creepy-crawly approach from the bank or, possibly more effective, a very careful wading technique working upstream with an absolute minimum of fuss or disturbance. Wading certainly allows for accurate presentation and less chance of a snag up.

dawn. We experience profound pleasures that other sportsmen can't even begin to imagine.

We are privileged and we know it, but with the privilege comes responsibility. I wouldn't even begin to preach about collecting litter or shutting gates, because I know such acts are instinctively part of us all, but let's just think about the fish for a moment, a creature so wild, so noble, so beautiful, and so graceful, and yet so often misunderstood or ignored by the public at large. Do let us bear in mind that although, for us, fishing is the best fun of our lives, it's not so for the fish. Let's ensure that we tread as lightly as possible along our river banks and bring compassion and understanding to all we do there.

➤ ONE HAPPY AUTHOR
OK, this isn't the biggest grayling I've ever caught, but as the day and the water were crystal clear, I felt I'd done well to land this fish of around a pound. The fish were extraordinarily wary, and the only way I could pick them off was by abnormally long casting. Generally I like to hunt my grayling up close, but they just weren't having it this particular day.

◄ A HUGELY SATISFYING MOMENT
Ruben really persevered long and hard to catch this fine example of a taimen on the fly, a fish that is more commonly pursued with a lure or dead bait. With faith, there's no reason why virtually any fish that swims won't take a fly if the right pattern is presented in the right place, in the right way, at the right time.

THE CARING ANGLER'S CODE

• Use barbless hooks or flatten the barbs before fishing to make hook removal 10 times easier.

• Try to do without treble hooks as much as possible, even on spinners; they can do untold damage, especially in pairs.

• Always wet your hands before touching a fish.

• If at all possible, unhook the fish in the water and let it swim free without ever leaving its own environment.

• If you do have to bring a fish into the air and onto the land, make sure it's kept in a wet landing net, put on an unhooking mat, and never left to writhe on hard gravel, stone, or a sandy beach.

• Never lift a fish by the tail, as this will disrupt its skeletal structure and condemn it to a lingering death.

• Only weigh and photograph important specimens. If you need to do so, make sure each function is carried out on the waterline itself. Keep a very careful check on the amount of time each exercise is taking.

• If a fish is tired after its struggle, support it in the shallows with its head facing upriver so that oxygen can pass through its gills. Do not move the fish backward and forward believing this will help the flow of water through its mouth; all you're doing is causing it further distress. Let the fish breathe naturally, and it will swim away in its own time.

• Don't be greedy. If you can, catch a couple of fish from a shoal and move on to another challenge. Once you've caught enough fish, pack it in for the day. Fish experience mental stress as well as physical pain.

• If you are going to take a fish for the table, pick a male rather than a female. This applies especially to female salmon whose eggs are so precious. Don't take more than you need, and let's see an end to fish-laden freezers.

• Fishing is a sport in which you can take pride. Let's be proud of ourselves and the way we play it.

PREPARATION

Preparing for an actual fishing trip should be regarded as both necessary and fun. Time spent planning the approaches, learning about the particular water, and preparing the right tackle is all part of the buildup to a successful campaign.

KNOWING THE FISH

JUST BY BEING A FLY ANGLER YOU ARE MAKING A STATEMENT—YOU
ARE IN THE BUSINESS OF BECOMING A FISHER-NATURALIST. YOUR JOB
IS TO PRESENT AS CLOSE AN IMITATION OF A NATURAL FOOD SOURCE
IN THE MOST PERFECT WAY POSSIBLE TO WHAT IS OFTEN A WILD
AND SUSPICIOUS FISH. TO DO SUCH A THING SUCCESSFULLY IN THE
HUNDREDS OF DIFFERENT SITUATIONS YOU WILL FACE TAKES THOUGHT.

Each and every challenge needs to be regarded calmly and rationally, and a whole host of considerations must be taken into account—what worked yesterday might not work today.

The world of nature is never static. Everything about the water and the fish that live in it is volatile and constantly changing. Our lives are comparatively ordered because of the comforts that civilization brings to us. If it's cold, we switch on the heat. If it's too hot, we turn on the air conditioning. Whatever food we might like is almost always available

to us. We are protected from the vagaries and uncertainties of the natural world. Bear in mind that this is not the case for the fish, which are constantly pulled here and there by changes in the environment around them.

Key Elements

Food and security are just about the only considerations that enter a fish's mind when it is not spawning time. The multitude of considerations that cross our own minds is absolutely irrelevant. A fish wants to live—that's all—and

that's where feeding plays such a vital part. Some fish that you pursue will be quite broad in their tastes and take anything edible in a random manner, but fishing is rarely as easy as this. In most cases, you will find it vital to get close to what your target fish is eating. For example, if trout are on the mayfly, little else will tempt them; sea trout can become preoccupied with elvers and refuse everything else; or you might find that bass want nothing but crabs.

You can find out what the fish you want to catch are feeding on

◄ ONE OF THE WORLD'S MYSTERIES
If people knew more about char and if char were more widely spread, then I have no doubt they would be among the top of the fly-fisher's quarries. They are beautiful, not easy to outwit, and fight with heart-stopping tenacity.

➤ AMERICA'S FAVORITE
Anybody who has fished for black bass will know within hours why they are just about the favorite fly-fishing target in the United States. A largemouth bass like this is supremely cunning, and this particular specimen took me a full four hours to outwit. In the end it fell for a small crab pattern. It was inched across the bottom, and the take, when it came, was so gentle the line merely flickered.

by observation or by trial and error. What you've got to learn to do is use your eyes. You'll certainly need polarizing glasses to strip away the reflections on the surface of the water so that your gaze can penetrate right down to where the fish are feeding. You might find binoculars are useful, too, to bring everything into a sharper, clearer focus. You'll need time and you'll need patience. Don't rush into presenting the wrong fly in an impetuous way, or you might find you have blown your chances completely.

Temperature

Bear in mind the water temperature and, if you care to, ascertain it with total accuracy by using a thermometer. There are some broad generalizations about water temperature that it's worth bearing

in mind. If the water is warm, most fish will be more active, as they are cold-blooded and their body temperature changes with their surroundings. In warm water you might well find fish mobile and feeding hard, but be warned—the water only has to get a degree or two above the optimum temperature for the fish to feel discomfort and begin to drift off the feed. Perhaps you can keep them interested with smaller food items presented in a more sophisticated way.

Cold water, too, can suppress the fishes' appetite, and falling temperatures can make them all but comatose. Once again, small food items might be the answer, or perhaps something large and colorful to trigger an aggressive response. There's no simple answer. You've simply got to think the problem through and try different

approaches until you find a solution. There's no point in fishing mechanically or thoughtlessly.

Water Clarity

Take into consideration the color of the water you are fishing, whether it be a river or a still water. Crystal-clear water can be good, because you can see the fish and what they're feeding upon with comparative ease, but, of course, the fish will be able to see you, and any clumsiness in your approach, with extreme clarity. Your leader and fly line will also show up

⋎ HIGH DRAMA
There is no such thing as a steelhead-fishing situation that isn't dramatic, but when there is snow in the air and ice along the margins of the river, then the sport assumes a heroism of its own. Richard Gibbs, a noted British angler, is seen here with a fine, fly-caught steelhead taken in the middle of a blizzard—a fishing situation he will never forget.

starkly. The situation is less demanding if there's a tinge of color in the water—the deficiencies in your approach and methods will be masked to a degree. If the water is very murky, then the chances are the fish won't see you or your tackle, but they might not see the fly either. Opt for something colorful that grabs their attention.

Currents

Rivers obviously have currents, but so, too, do stillwaters, and these become more noticeable the larger the water. On really big lakes, especially after a wind, there can be real pushes and pulls of water beneath the surface. Currents are important to all fish—often they

⋏ SPRING CREEKS

The "typical" fly-fisherman's river just does not exist. Each and every one has its own individual character and, no matter how expert you are, you still need to take time to work out how a new water behaves. Spring creeks like this tend to be up and down like a fiddler's elbow according to weather conditions. Food stocks are comparatively unstable and the fish tend to move lies frequently, making spring creeks fascinating places to fish.

➤ CHALK STREAM DELIGHT

Of all trout rivers the chalk stream is generally considered the ultimate, almost the cradle of trout-fishing civilization! This is a shot of a beautifully preserved piece of water with abundant weed growth and an astonishingly healthy larder of insect life. The trout here are browns, and they're wild and self-perpetuating.

like to lie facing them so that they receive an ample supply of oxygen. The currents also bring them food, such as insects, drifting helplessly along and just waiting to be eaten. When fish decide to move, they'll often go with the current simply to save on energy. Think, too, how the current affects the way you present a fly. It can catch your line, form a bow and make your imitation behave unnaturally. Water is rarely a still, dead element—it's all about fluid movement, and we need to understand its many dimensions.

Light

Fish cannot control the light levels around them. Their lidless eyes are at the mercy of the weather, and they often find scorching bright light uncomfortable. Frequently, they'll go very deep or, if the water is shallow, they'll look for cover, perhaps in weeds, under lily pads, or beneath an overhanging tree. In these conditions, they may only begin to feed at dusk, or even well into the night. Sea trout and Arctic char are perfect examples of this. However, if the light is more somber, most fish will feed throughout the day, especially if

▲ CONTENTMENT
Does life get much better? A glorious sunset, a calm evening, a plentiful hatch of fly, and steadily rising trout. You have the whole world, seemingly, to yourself.

there's consistent cloud cover and perhaps a sprinkling of rain. A wind can improve the fishing when conditions are dull, but on a bright day the ripples can refract the light and intensify it, putting the fish off.

Weather Forecasts

You can see from all the above just how important the weather is to the fish, and what an impact it has on the waters that they inhabit. It's important to keep an eye on the weather and to consider how changes might affect your sport. For example, the onset of a low pressure system can be a bad thing, because fish generally enjoy stable weather and a well-ordered lifestyle. On the other hand, an extended period of high pressure can mean the weather becomes hotter and hotter, and this will cause the fish to become more and more lethargic. It's then that the approach of wind and rain can revitalize them by pumping fresh oxygen into the water. Watch the weather and its changes, and observe how the fish respond. Build up your own picture of the waters that you fish, because each and every environment reacts in a unique fashion.

Territory

Most fish have their own territorial ranges. We talk about a trout having a lie, a place where it knows food will come to it and where it feels secure. Often trout will stay in the same lie for months on end until a bigger fish, angling pressure, or violent changes in weather conditions force it to move. Other fish have larger territories, especially coastal sea fish that follow the tides, but you'll find that even these regularly come back to the same lie. It's important to watch your fish, to analyze its movements, and to work out where best to put that cast so that your fly will be seen to greatest advantage.

➤ NEW HORIZONS

In the past 50 years, the fly has led the angler to all manner of countries to meet up with all manner of exotic fish species. None is more exciting than the bonefish found in The Bahamas. Bonefish might not be large, but there is no faster swimming sport fish. If you don't let them go on that first searing run then you're simply courting disaster.

Keep On Learning

I know how tempting it is to simply buy your gear and a huge collection of flies, dash out, and immediately start fishing, but don't. Always take the time to get to know the fish and attempt to work out what they will be doing on any given occasion. This isn't boring—it is fundamental to the sport of fly fishing. Fish are not a commodity to be picked up effortlessly from a superstore shelf—they are living, vibrant creatures with distinct life patterns all their own.

Every fish in the world can be caught on fly, and the chances are you will fish for different species in different waters, perhaps on different continents. You'll never stop learning—there are so many different factors that will influence whether a fish will take that fly or not. It's a fascinating quest that you are embarking upon. Sometimes the key information is well-known. For example, a lot of late summer trout feed on banks of tiny organisms called daphnia, and these rise and fall according to the light. On dull days they come nearer to the surface, but you'll need to fish deep in bright conditions.

Then again, you'll be told by everyone that salmon generally wait in the sea until high water swells the rivers, letting them pass up easily and unobserved, but there are exceptions. A couple of years ago, high winds pushed a school of dolphins into an English bay. The salmon were there waiting for a flood, but the big mammals so terrorized them that they fled up a river that was still low and clear. Pulse after pulse of fish flocked upriver, forced on by this most unusual of circumstances. As you can see, fly fishing brings you right to the core, the nerve center of nature. A large part of the fun lies in catching a fish but, if you're wise, you'll discover that knowledge can be just as stimulating—and without knowledge, you'll never become a successful fly fisher.

◄ RECONNAISSANCE
If you want to fail, get to the water as quickly as you can, throw up your tackle, and immediately begin fishing. That way you're pretty well guaranteed to go home fishless. Instead, leave your rod in its bag and simply walk the banks, all the while watching exactly where the fish are and upon what they are feeding. Chat to fellow anglers—you'll generally find them most forthcoming. Then sit down, make your plans, and with quiet deliberation set about the task of fishing.

DISTINGUISHING FEATURES

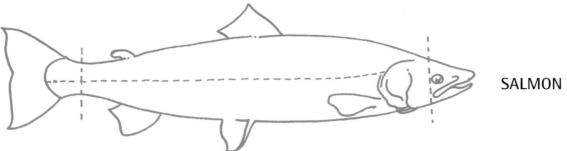

SALMON

The sea trout's upper jaw reaches well past the hind edge of the eye. The salmon's upper jaw reaches only to the hind margin of the eye.

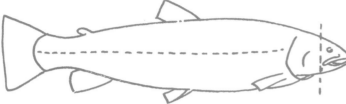

SEA TROUT

It is often important for fishery management to be able to differentiate between trout and salmon parr. In brown trout parr, the tip of the adipose fin and the edge of the pectorals are red. In salmon parr, the adipose fin is slate-colored. As in adult fish, the position of the eye relative to the end of the jaw is also important. It is also unusual in salmon parr for there to be any red spots below the lateral line.

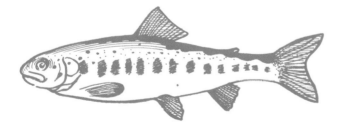

SALMON PARR

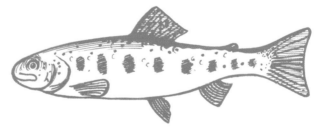

TROUT PARR

The tail in salmon and sea trout varies enormously. When relaxed, the tail of a big sea trout is straight but when stretched it becomes convex. The salmon's tail is more concave with two horns top and bottom. The base of a salmon's tail is also thinner with a pronounced wrist. The sea trout's broader-based tail has no wrist.

SALMON TAIL

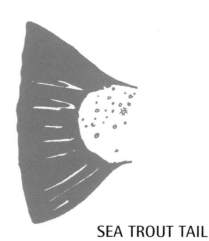

SEA TROUT TAIL

WATERCRAFT

It's very easy to put too much reliance on false gods in fishing. Tackle, fly choice, and presentation are all important but, as a starting point, you've got to consider the fish and the waters they inhabit. When faced with any fishing situation, the key is to take your time and not to rush to make that first cast.

Sit and watch. Show patience. Merge into the life and pace of the water. Shed your outside life. Focus entirely on the fishing situation in front of you. A picture of the water will begin to emerge that was previously invisible, and eventually you'll become one with the task in front of you.

Observation is the Key

Among the most essential tools are your eyes. Learn to use them and to interpret accurately the information they feed you. However, your naked eyes are not enough—they need help. You must, as a serious fly fisherman, invest in a pair of polarizing glasses, binoculars, and chest waders. I've got more to say about these vital accessories in the next chapter. A logbook is also a particularly good idea. The information that you're building up is hard-earned, and it's vital not to lose it.

Starting on a Still Water

Be the lake large or small, the rules are the same. Try, if at all possible, to find a vantage point from which

> SPRINGTIME
Even in springtime, before the water has truly warmed and flies become abundant, it is still important to look carefully at a river and learn from your deductions. Look for depressions in the riverbed, where food items—and fish—are likely to congregate. Learn to read a river and you will soon reap the rewards.

you can see as much as possible of the water that you're intending to fish. A hill or a tall building are perfect places to begin. Get an overall impression of the water and its shape. Consider the prevailing wind. On a lake where the wind is likely to come from the southwest, the northeast corner is likely to produce some of the best fishing, simply because of the food that's pushed there. This isn't always the case, but it's frequently so.

◄ VIEW FROM A BRIDGE
No true angler can pass by a bridge without stopping and staring—and to good effect. Stand on a bridge and let the whole tempo of the river sink into your psyche. How is the river flowing? What flies are emerging? Are the fish feeding hard or lethargically? Are they in the light or the shade? Should you fish now or simply pass the time until the light begins to fade and your chances improve?

The next task, long before you start fishing, is to get some impression of the various depths. You'll really need to know these, as in very hot, clear weather the fish will be down deep, while in cloudy, choppy conditions you're more likely to find them in shallow margins.

It's also important to investigate weed growth. Some weed types are particularly attractive to fish—lilies, for example. Weeds obviously offer shade, protection, and food. Look also for any other features—islands and overhanging trees are particularly favored. Perhaps a dam wall, a spring, or an inflowing stream will attract the fish. Keep in mind that fish aren't scattered randomly throughout the water.

They'll be attracted to particular areas for specific reasons.

If the water is clear enough, set yourself to watch individual fish and try to work out their patrol routes. Soon you'll build up a picture of how certain fish are moving and where you can best put a fly without raising their suspicions.

There are those who regard still-water fly fishing as dull and uninteresting, but this is only because they haven't taken the time to really study the water in front of them and build up a complete mental picture of it. Stillwaters reveal their secrets slowly, and serious study will find your catches improving greatly. Of course, you can set up and fish blind, perhaps stripping a big lure

⋏ WATCHING THE WATER

The angler here is scrutinizing the gravels beneath a bridge pool. He's looking for any predominant source of potential food—hatching flies, an undue number of shrimp, beetles, or caddis grubs. A river as tiny and clear as this can give all manner of clues as to the right approach. Once a decision is made, it will be an upstream cast, snaking the line under the bridge into the deep, placid water that spells security for a big trout.

back toward you, and you'll catch fish—but you won't catch the biggest fish and you won't catch fish consistently. You also probably won't know why you caught them, and that is to side-step the challenge that fly fishing presents.

SIGHTING FISH

There is a skill to seeing fish. Their lives depend on perfect camouflage. They can only survive by being nearly invisible to herons, ospreys, cormorants—and us—so they are not going to stand out starkly like goldfish in a garden pond. So what are the rules of the game? Well, this is what works for me.

First of all, make yourself comfortable, relax, and simply watch the water in front of you. Let yourself fall into a kind of trance. Don't try to focus intently. Just let the water in front of you seep into your subconscious. Keep this up for a while, and sooner or later something will attract your attention and make you focus your gaze. It may be a gleam of color, a shape crossing a gravel bar, or a weed frond suddenly transforming itself into a waving fin. It will happen. A fish will eventually move its body, reflect or obstruct the light, and signal its presence.

Once you've seen that initial tell-tale sign, really focus in on the area. Scorch the water with your eyes. Soon you will begin to make out the entire fish—its shape, its position, its size, its species—and you'll wonder why you didn't see it sooner.

Now, and only now, are you ready to start formulating a plan, deciding where you're going to place your fly and how deeply it's got to sink to fall into the feeding zone. If you'd rushed in and begun to cast without seeing the fish, you would only have succeeded in frightening it out of its territory, rendering it impossible to catch.

⅄ INVISIBLE
These small warm-water fish are almost invisible to predators... apart from that giveaway black eye—their one undoing. When choosing a fly, bear characteristics such as this in mind and look for patterns that emit a subtle signal, a target for predators to home in on.

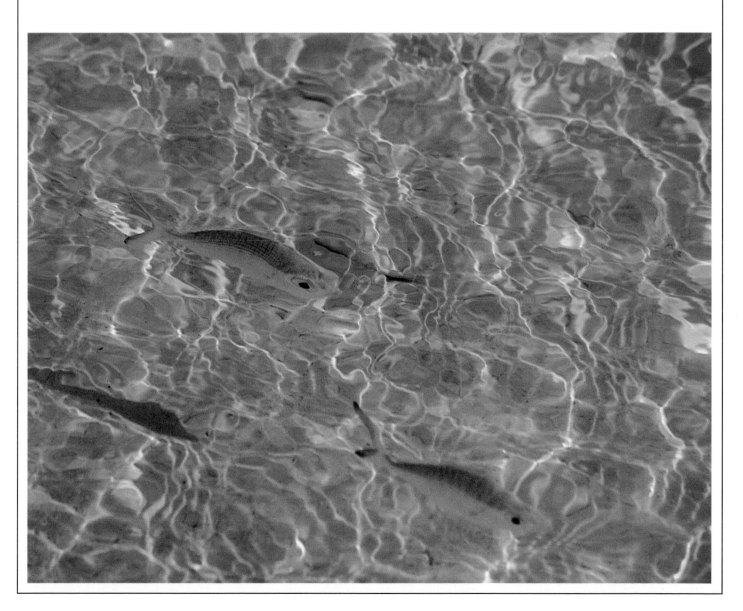

A DREAM POOL

The wider and deeper the stretch of river, the more difficult it is to read it with absolute precision. Remember that the currents will have a very unexpected life of their own and that water moves faster near the surface than it does down toward the bottom. This can be problematic when you're trying to work a fly down deep at a naturally-paced speed.

Discovering the River

Much of the same advice applies when you are river fishing. If the river is new to you, walk the length of your beat before considering putting up your tackle. Walk slowly and study the water in front of you minutely. Once again, look for any features, particularly depth changes, bends, currents that reveal the presence of underwater structures. Again, watch for individual fish, either lying quietly or actively "on the fin" and feeding. Select fish that you'd like to go back to and try to catch. This is the art of river fishing: pinpointing target fish and not just fishing blindly or indiscriminately.

Remember that there are always reasons why fish adopt a certain lie or patrol route. Every aspect of their behavior has a cause. Work out the complex patterns of their lives, and you'll be in a position to catch them.

WEIGHING IT UP

Stan is one of the best guides on the southern English chalk streams, and here he's talking Mindy, an American angler, through the strategy on a sweeping bend. It's late in the season and there's not a huge amount of fly life around, but the trout are still hungry and preparing for spawning, which isn't too far off. Nymphs work well, but they've got to be presented at exactly the right depth and move as naturally with the current as possible. It's no use just casting blind. Mark your fish, watch its feeding pattern, and assess exactly where you're going to have to cast the fly so the two coincide. This is a mind game and a mental puzzle just as much as it is a physical sport.

HAWK-EYE

If you don't know a pool, take the time to stare into it intently to work out the rhythm of the currents, any boulders, fallen trees or other snags, and, especially, where fish might actually be lying. A single planned cast is worth a hundred haphazard ones.

The Hunter's Rules

There are a few golden rules to follow when approaching any water if you are to maximize your chances.

Firstly, always watch your footfall. Sound travels approximately five times more clearly through water than it does through air, and this is a very big deal if you're trying not to spook the fish. The crunch of a boot on gravel really does have an impact and can set the fish on their guard long before you think of making a cast. A frightened fish is a wary fish, and a wary fish is difficult to catch. Be aware of the ground on which you're walking. Stone and gravel transmit sound much more clearly than grass or mud, but even these can present problems as they're frequently soft and unstable, and

➢ WICKED WATER

Really fast water like this is by far best fished by the wading angler. You can get directly in line with your flies so there is no bend in the line that you have to worry about constantly mending. You're direct to the business end and you're going to feel every single take, no matter how slight. However, never wade in fast water past the depth where you feel comfortable. A wading staff is a good aid.

⅄ INTO A FISH

So, Simon's wading antics have paid off and he's now playing a very healthy fish indeed that punches heavier than its weight in such a quick current. It's very tempting to follow a fish in quick water like this, but resist it if at all possible. If you start splashing after a fish, there's always a chance that you could trip, fall, and get into real trouble. You're also disturbing more water downriver of you. If possible, dig in, give line grudgingly, wait for the fish to tire, and then pull it toward the margin where the current is less strong.

send out vibrations that again give your game away. The simple solution is to try and mimic the stealthy heron!

Keep your voice down, too. In shallow water especially, or when fish are lying near the surface,

there's absolutely no doubt that a strident voice is heard and noted, and again your chances will dip alarmingly. If you must talk to a friend, do so in low tones. If the fish is very close to you, then whisper. You're not being melodramatic—

⋏ BROKEN WATER

This is the perfect water for the wet-fly fisherman. Explore the pockets of water hidden behind rocks and under weirs and waterfalls. Keep on the move: a cast here, a cast there, and then flick onto another spot entirely. In such water, trout are always on the fin and move quickly when they see something they like.

CAPITALIZING ON THE COMMOTION

Watch the life around the waterside carefully, and you will quickly realize that other creatures use the bankside apart from you and that the fish aren't frightened of them. This is worth noting, because it's often possible to get close to spooky fish in the shadow of creatures that don't alarm them.

Cattle frequently come down to the water to drink and the fish take no notice,

so get in among them and you'll find you can watch spooked fish much more closely.

As the cattle drink, they stir up the mud with their hooves and send colored water downstream. Fish will often come in to investigate, looking for items of disturbed food, and the colored water will mask your line and your presence.

A fleet of swans appears around the bend feeding hard on weeds. They're

making a lot of noise and disturbing the water. Now you can get in downstream of the swans and cast for fish that have become much less able to detect your presence. The swans will also have uprooted a good deal of weeds, releasing unexpected food supplies, and the fish will be feeding hard on all manner of insects. Here's a golden chance to offer your fly to fish whose appetite is already awakened.

◀ A COUNTRY STREAM

This is a different water altogether. It twists and meanders through heavy woodland, and you're going to find plenty of places where the trout like to lie up. Look for them in deeper pools, amid lengths of ranunculus weed, and on bends where the trees crowd over, giving shade from the sunlight and security from aerial predators. A lot of your casting is going to be very tight and precise. Don't put out too long a line and be aware of any sneaky winds.

you're simply being sensible. Don't call across the river to your friend, or shout from one boat to another. Sound travels clearly across water and the fish will be picking it all up. The chances are, they won't like a word you're saying!

On a river, you should walk upstream in order to approach fish from behind. This way you are less likely to disturb them, but you should also try to avoid scaring small fish in the margins. If scared, these will dart out into mid-river and spread the message of your

arrival among the bigger fish. You're an alien presence in the fish's world, so minimize your impact.

Watch your shadow. When you're peering into the water, try to use bankside cover so that it merges with the shadow of a tree or tall grasses and reeds. There's no shame in walking at a stoop, or even crawling, if you think the situation demands it. The guy stomping around bolt upright with a braying voice is the one who will go home fishless, not you. Be especially aware of your shadow as the sun sinks, throwing it further out across the stream.

Think carefully about your camouflage, about how you can merge into the surroundings. Your clothing should be drab. You'll chance upon many "tackle tarts" along the riverbank, with shining gadgets pinned to every lapel and pocket. These may look good to humans, but they undoubtedly catch the light and reflect a warning to the fish.

Think about your face and the effect when the sun strikes it. If you have ever dived, you'll know exactly what I mean. Otherwise, take my word for it. A hat with a broad brim casts a shadow that makes your face much less bright and alarming.

It's nice to have the latest rod with a dazzling lacquer finish, but watch it in the sunlight as you cast and see how it flashes out danger. What's wrong with a matt finish if you can find one? All these little things count.

✙ DON'T SPOOK THE FISH

I can't overemphasize the need for a careful approach in tiny waters. If the fish sense anything wrong—even a slight footfall—then they'll be off, and all you will see is a cloud of silt where they've accelerated from zero. And I'm not too sure about that hat. The jacket is OK, but anything that stands out from a drab background is suspect. Notice, however, that I'm keeping well back from the water's edge. Always keep a good margin of vegetation between you and the water.

FLY-FISHING TACKLE

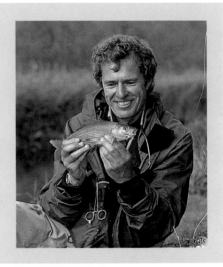

YOU HAVE NO DOUBT REALIZED THAT THERE IS NO SUCH THING AS AN OUTFIT FOR ALL FLY-FISHING SITUATIONS. THE RIGHT ROD AND REEL FOR A TINY MOORLAND STREAM CERTAINLY WON'T BE ENOUGH TO PURSUE ATLANTIC OR PACIFIC SALMON ON A MIGHTY RIVER. THAT MUCH IS OBVIOUS, BUT HOW DO YOU DECIDE WHAT KIND OF SETUP YOU ACTUALLY NEED?

The obvious starting point is to consider the type of fishing you'll most often engage in and buy the gear to suit that. Thereafter, during the course of your fishing career, you can add outfits as you travel and build up fresh experiences. Before moving on to greater detail, though, I will say this, albeit in hushed tones. I have a particular 9-foot rod rated 5/6-weight, which is allied to a 6-weight floating line, and this combination suits me for at least 80 per cent of the fishing that I personally enjoy, be it on streams, rivers, or stillwaters. I can enjoy the fight of a 12-ounce

trout and still have the confidence to land an 8-pound salmon. It's certainly not the ideal rod for everything, but in many, many cases it will just about do. I realize the tackle trade won't be very keen on this particular admission, so I'll hurry on to more conventional comments.

Before we proceed, you need to know about the weight rating system. All rods, whatever their length, are classified by the weight of line they ideally cast. There's some latitude in this, but it's comparatively narrow. The line weight is based on the long-held

ASFA system formulated by the American Sport Fishing Association many years ago. This means that an 8-foot rod designated 7-weight is more powerful than an 8-foot rod rated 4-weight. The higher the number, the heavier the line the rod can cast.

So, having dealt with this essential complication, we can move onto more interesting subjects. Let's begin with length. At 7 feet, a rod is really only suitable for brooks, streams, and smaller rivers. Your casting range is necessarily limited, and you'll probably be looking to harness the rod with a 3- or 4-

◅ BASS DELIGHT
Like many fish, bass can be taken on fly, bait, and lure, but most would agree that fly fishing is the most thrilling and sporting method of the three. It's also uniquely flexible. Fish for bass on the top with little popper flies, or deep on the bottom with creepy-crawly nymphs, or at any level between with fish imitations. The list of approaches is endless.

➤ A TENSE MOMENT
Don has hooked a very nice trout and it's now struggling on the surface without the power to mount any more serious dives for freedom. The landing net now comes into play. Normally Don might not bother with a net, but here the thick reed growth between him and the water is too soft and swampy to risk putting all his weight onto and sinking into the mire. A net gives him the reach that he needs.

weight line. However, there are tremendous bonuses. A short rod is easier to work in undergrowth. It's also as light as a feather and can lay a thin line down with hardly any disturbance. Also, a short rod is supremely accurate when throwing a line out in tight loops to place a fly absolutely on the nose of a rising fish. You've also got to think of the aesthetics of what you're doing. No longer are we expected to feed a family with our catches—we go fishing to enjoy ourselves, and 7-footers are all about fun, feel, and intimacy. An 8-ounce trout wouldn't seem much on a salmon rod, but on a 7-footer you can expect the scrap of your life!

At 8 feet (plus a few inches, perhaps), you are stepping up significantly. With a rod of this length, probably attached to a 5- or 6-weight line, you can be reasonably confident of fishing small to medium-sized rivers and even small stillwaters. The rod will probably have a fair bit of punch to it, and you'll be able to hammer out a line into a brisk wind. There'll be more spine to the rod, too, when it comes to playing a fish, and larger trout or even small summer salmon aren't totally beyond you with gear like this. Of course, an 8-footer is still light, still a joy to fish with, and still casts with supreme accuracy.

Moving Up

Once you reach 9 feet, you're really moving the goal posts. As I've already guiltily confessed, a 9-foot rod teamed with a 6-weight line does me for most fly-fishing situations. For example, I'm happy fishing for grayling with it, trout in

⩒ GOOD FISH RUNNING

Ruben's into a cracker here. A big fish has taken his fly, turned broadside to the current, and is off at a pace. All the loose line in the current in front of him will be whipped away as the trout continues to motor off. Then Ruben will be able to play the fish from the reel in classic style. Don't worry too much, therefore, about slack line around you, providing it doesn't get caught up around underwater snags or, particularly, your legs.

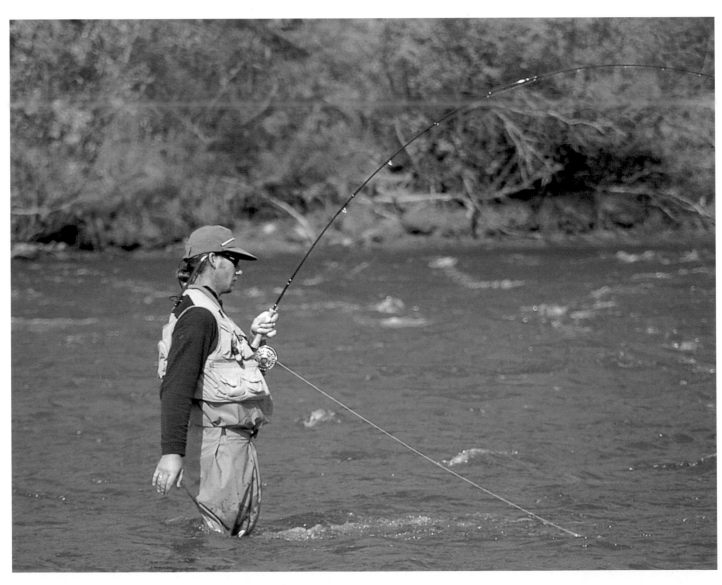

STANDARD FISHING TACKLE

1 HAT *A broad brim shades your face, keeps the sun out of your eyes, and lets you watch the water more easily.*

2 POLARIZING GLASSES *These are especially essential when fishing sub-surface with nymphs or wet flies. You'll often see the fish actually take the fly and you'll find that your hooking ratio rockets.*

3 BAG *Useful for all your gear.*

4 CLUB *Releases fish humanely.*

5 NYLON *Line in various strengths to make up your own leaders and tippet.*

6 FLOATANT *Keeps dry flies afloat.*

7 BINOCULARS *Light binoculars can help you see what type of flies are hatching. They also enable you to scan the river far and wide, helping you to pick up fish that*

are rising beyond the range of the naked eye. They also, obviously, help you enjoy the bird life up and down the river.

8 HEMOSTAT *This is necessary to slip the hook out of the catch's mouth.*

9 LINE FLOATANT *Keeps line afloat.*

10 LEADERS *Ready-made tapered leaders are more expensive than those you can make on the bankside. But they do lay a fly over beautifully and cause a minimum of disturbance. They're invaluable, therefore, for clear water and spooked fish.*

11 MULTI-TOOL *Don't weigh yourself down with too many gadgets, but this is an essential tool. Clippers are much better than teeth for tidying up knots. Also, a small metal spike can be invaluable for piercing a fly hook eye that's gummed up*

with varnish from the tying process. Items like this are best secured on retractors that clip to a fishing vest or jacket and give instant access.

12 STRIKE INDICATORS *These are essential for controlling the depth your nymph fishes at. They are also vital for an instant visual indication of a take. However, do check that the fishery rules allow their use.*

13 VARIOUS FLIES *Worldwide there are tens of thousands of fly patterns. Ensure that you have a good selection of nymphs, wet flies, dry flies, lures, and, if necessary, salmon flies. Look after them and keep them secure in a damp-proof box. Don't let them become dislodged and rattle about, or the hook points will get damaged.*

any sort of river, smaller stillwaters, and even Arctic char in Greenland. Nine feet is perfect for a river rod, and there's very little moving water that will be beyond it. You'll also be able to fish many of the smaller stillwaters with confidence, though you'll probably be out-gunned on larger lakes and reservoirs. A heavy sinking line would also be taxing it to the limit, but for a floating or intermediate line the 9-footer is incredibly versatile.

Some companies make 10-foot rods to attach to a 4- or 5-weight line, which is perfect for the Czech nymph technique, of which you will read more later. This method demands

pinpoint control, and that is what those extra 2 feet give you. Whether from boat or bank, the 10-footer can open up a huge amount of fishing to you and is only really out of place on the smaller waters with the lightest of lines for comparatively modest fish.

⋏ SPECTACULAR STEELHEAD

In the view of many, the steelhead, especially fresh-run from the sea, is just about the most dramatic fly fisherman's quarry that exists. A big fresh fish like this fights with a ferocity that is difficult to imagine. You can take them on spinners or egg baits, but they are happy to come to flies, often large ones skated across the surface imitating moths or large, struggling insects.

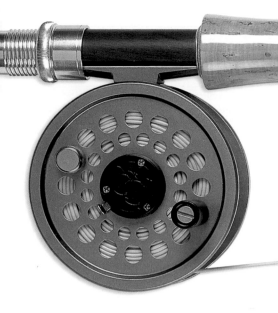

YOUR NEW ROD
When you're choosing a rod make sure that you hold it and flex it and, if possible, actually use it in a real fishing situation. The rod should be well-balanced and the handle fit very snugly into your grasp. Don't forget to take off the plastic protective wrapping, or the cork will sweat and damage.

Salmon, Steelhead, and Salt

An 11-footer simply takes the 10-footer up the range in terms of power: you can fish further and heavier. You have added control in foul weather conditions. You have a bit more guts to deal with a larger salmon or perhaps a steelhead. Above 11 feet and you are really moving into the designated salmon rod. These generally begin at 13 feet, but go right through to 15 or even 16 feet. You'll find them coupled with 8- to 11-weight lines, and they are generally designed for double-handed casting, often the Spey cast. Once upon a time, rods of this length were astoundingly heavy, being made of bamboo or greenheart. Today, thanks to graphite, even a rod that seems to go on forever can still be light, crisp, and a joy to use.

Which length do you want for your salmon rod? Well, a great deal depends on your own physique, on the type of river you're fishing, and, to some degree, the time of the year. If you're fishing the summer on smaller rivers, then probably a 13-footer allied with a floating 9-weight line will be adequate. If, however, you're fishing a raging winter river, when you've got to get flies down really deep, then it's probably wise to go for a 15-footer and a sinking 10-weight. Think it out carefully: don't rush into the wrong choice.

There are also many specialized rods around: there have even been rods designed to take a 0-weight line… you wonder whether it might defy gravity and never actually land on the water!

If the saltwater scene attracts you, you can easily find 9- or 10-foot rods capable of shooting out 9- or 10-weight lines. These offer the powerful action needed to cast into

⋏ BALANCE
The key to successful fly casting is tackle in complete harmony. The fly line must complement the rod precisely. The reel should be of a compatible weight. Your leader should not be overly long and should be exactly the right diameter both for the fly that you're casting and for the fish that you're hoping to land. Nothing must be out of tune if you're going to get the very best fishing rhythm.

◄ PERFECTLY HOOKED
A trout doesn't come better hooked than this, neatly pricked in the top lip the instant it sucked in the nymph. For easy release, hooks can be barbless, but the point must be sharp as most fish are lost through missing the take or not setting the hook.

high winds, and also have the power to fight a big permit as it heads down into deep water. You might also consider gear like this for a jaunt after pike or muskie. In short, whatever your desires, there will be a rod out there to suit you. Just take the time to make sure you locate the right beast for your purpose.

There are other considerations, too. Do you like the feel of the rod? Looks shouldn't be important but, inevitably, they are, so does it really appeal to you? After all, choosing a fishing rod is like taking a partner: you hope it will be for life. Ensure that the handle feels comfortable in your grasp. Are the corks top quality? If not, they'll break down under repeated use. Is the reel seat a really secure screw fitting? Are the rod rings light but strong—double-legged if necessary? The matter of how many pieces the rod breaks down into is of vital importance if you're a traveler. For example, you can take a 4-piece 10-foot rod onto a plane with you and eliminate those heart-stopping moments at the baggage claim. Does the rod come with a strong tube to protect it from knocks? Is there a lifetime guarantee? That's something you really should be demanding these days. Read reviews, talk to anglers on the bank, and don't just take the word of a tackle dealer who might be trying to get rid of last year's unwanted stock.

➤ ASLAM'S DELIGHT
Aslam is an Indian boy who was hired originally to scare monkeys from the camp, but he took to fly fishing magnificently. The gear he is holding is traditional salmon tackle, which on this occasion was pressed into service for the mighty mahseer of the southern Indian rivers. It worked well at first, but finally collapsed under the power of what was probably a 70- or 80-pound fish.

Choosing a Fly Reel

Once upon a time, fly reels were nothing but reservoirs for the line, and they would clatter like a bag of wrenches if put under any pressure from the fish. Their drag systems were atrocious and, in short, they were pretty undesirable objects. Even today, there are a lot of suspect reels on the market. A simple test is to pick up any prospective purchase, hold it by the spool, and shake it. If there's any wobble, however slight, you can bet it will quickly get worse.

Modern reels give you just about everything. The large arbor reels, with their wide-looped storage, make for incredibly low line memory and all but eradicate those irritating coils. They also make retrieving line that much faster. Drag systems are also much improved. Look for one that is easily adjustable and offers "low start-up inertia", meaning that it doesn't need an enormous tug to get the spool moving—perfect if you're fishing light leaders. Look for a reel that is suited to the line you'll be using, that is light, fits your prospective rod like a glove, and has a really strong, integrated reel seat. Most reels are made of graphite or top-quality aluminum. If you're choosing aluminum, make sure it is anodized if you intend to do any sea fishing, or it will corrode.

The Fly Line

As we have seen in the discussion of rods, there are different types of fly line as well as different weights. Some fly lines are meant to float, others to hang just under the surface film, and others to sink at differing rates. For example, if you're trying to get a fly down as deep and as quickly as possible, then you'll go for a fast sinker. If you want to slowly explore the depths, then you'll go for a slow sinker. Most still-water fly fishermen, especially these days, have a whole armory of different lines stored away on separate spools that are interchangeable. This can be important: you may arrive at the lake early in the morning and find a flat calm with fish taking from the surface. You'll obviously rig up a floating line and either a dry fly or perhaps something fished in the film.

The day clouds over, a wind begins to rise. There's nothing showing on the surface and you've got to get down deeper. This is where a sinking line is important. Or let's say the day continues bright. The heat increases as the sun rises, and the fish drop ever closer to the bottom. Now you've got to pursue them in the depths and a fast sinker is called for. The sun sinks. The wind dies. Once again, as evening approaches, the fish are on the surface. Now you need that floating line again.

The decision isn't just about weight and where the line fishes in the water; there are also different line profiles. The most traditional is a double-taper, which has a significant belly and is thinner toward each end. This means it casts well and the line closest to the fish lands gently. The weight-forward lines are intended for medium- to long-distance casting, and once the tip and belly of the line have gone through, the thin running line passes easily through the rod rings. Shooting heads consist of short lengths of fly line backed by fine braid, which produces little resistance when flying through the rod rings. These are more advanced and are designed for very long-distance casting.

⊻ A LOVELY LINE

Simon is a skillful caster. Notice how his line uncoils beautifully and shoots out across the river toward its intended target. He has exactly the right, balanced tackle for the job, but his timing, too, is critical. He doesn't strain. He has a natural rhythm that is unflustered but powerful. Don't push for distance in the early days. Instead, make sure that you're hitting the target and your line lands with a minimum of fuss on the surface.

The Leader

The only other major consideration, apart from the flies (which deserve a chapter to themselves), is the leader that ties the fly to the fly line. Once upon a time, everyone used standard monofilament, but there are many different materials available now. Copolymer and fluorocarbon alternatives offer enhanced strengths at very low diameter, and are often a favorite choice. Do be careful, though: these modern lines can be abraded quickly by a big fish in a snaggy situation. My advice is to stick with standard nylon if you know you're going to be pulling a specimen from the snags. Leaders, by and large, should be tapered, getting thinner toward the fly. This means they turn over more easily in the air and land with minimal disturbance.

⅄ MAHSEER'S DOWNFALL
So, as you can see, the salmon tackle worked! This beautiful mahseer of around 12 pounds in weight fell for a big streamer fly fished in quick, white water and gave a tremendous 15-minute battle.

➢ FISHING ON TOP
This is a little surface-popping fly. Notice its blunt head: this pushes against the water film and creates a splashing, chugging type of motion that many fish find totally irresistible. Try using this kind of fly for large- or smallmouth bass. Due to its weight, it's not overly easy to cast, and an eight-weight rod would probably be more suitable than the seven-weight featured here.

◁ THE MASTER'S CHOICE
Aslam proved a natural fly fisher. Here he is going through my box of big flies, picking out something that he believes in. Of course, fly fishing for mahseer is not widely practiced, and there's a great deal of pioneering going on. These flies, incidentally, also work well for pike, barracuda, and any big predator.

Accessories

What else do you need? Well, sometimes you want to make a leader float or, alternatively, sink quickly. You can buy various sprays, pastes, and liquids to achieve these effects. You can also invest in one of the proprietary substances that help to make dry flies float more perkily and more bushy tailed than your own hot breath can ever achieve! A pair of sharp scissors is always a good idea, too, for snipping off unwanted ends, and of course you need a hemostat to slip the hook from a beaten fish's jaw.

You'll almost certainly need a landing net, but in every situation you should ask yourself whether you need to use it. You can often simply draw the fish to you, kneel by it, and flick the hook out without a net at all. This is much kinder on the fish,

as by keeping it in the water at all times the stress is hugely reduced.

We'll come across various other items of tackle as we progress through the book, but the one essential is polarizing glasses. These are one of your most important purchases for two reasons: the first and paramount one is safety. You simply cannot take the risk of fly fishing, especially in a wind, with your eyes unprotected. One momentary lapse of concentration, or a single unexpected gust of wind, and you could lose the sight of an eye. It's just not worth it.

Polarizing lenses are also your magical aid to seeing what is happening under the surface. The reflective glare of the water is stripped away and now you can see where fish are lying and often what they are feeding on. You can see the

▼ THE PERFECT PIKE KIT
Remember, whatever you're fishing for, always make sure that your spool is filled to the correct depth. This will almost always mean quite a considerable length of backing goes onto the drum before the fly line. This is important for two main reasons: you need

your fly line to be stored in the largest loops possible so that it does not kink. Secondly, if a big fish, such as an enraged 20-pound pike, runs you've just got to be able to give line, and that means backing. A bonefish, for example, will commonly take 100 yards of backing off the reel.

▼ DOES COLOR COUNT?
The question of fly line color has exercised anglers' minds for many years. There is the feeling that a very bright color can be picked up more easily by the fish, but generally a floating line is simply seen in silhouette at best. Perhaps when it comes to sinking lines, color is more of an issue. Of course, a highly visible floating line does have advantages for the angler. It's possible to see even the slightest take much more easily.

contours of the bed, the makeup of the weeds, and even the insects going about their everyday business. Without the glasses you can only guess at what's happening beneath the surface, and guesswork simply doesn't make for successful fishing.

Do you need a fishing bag or will a fishing vest carry everything you need for the day? The answer depends on the complexity of the fishing situation that awaits you. If, for example, you're fishing a river all day long for trout, then you really only need extra leader material and a fly box, so the vest is perfect. If, however, you're fishing a big match on a reservoir, then you probably need a whole array of spools, flies, and other assorted kit, which can only fit into a box or bag.

Gizmos

If you go into a major fly-fishing tackle store, then you will see endless amounts of bits and bobs on sale, but let's be straight about it—none of these is absolutely essential to success. Nevertheless, they've all been designed to help with a host of situations where problems can arise. My advice is to get yourself to the biggest fly-fisher's store that you can and devote a whole morning or afternoon to just browsing, looking at exactly what's on offer and thinking about its possible uses. Let's look at some examples.

You'll probably need sinkants of some sort or another whether you're fishing still or running water. A sinkant simply sinks your leader fast and true, and this is often necessary, especially when fishing very light flies. You might also consider buying some sinkant putty. This is lead-free and is created to mold either onto the line or around the head of the fly. You can therefore sink any fly much more quickly than normal. This can be very important in deep water or in swift currents.

You might need a proprietary leader straightener to iron out any little curls or loops in your leader, which can be very irritating and can damage your fly presentation. You might also consider buying braided leaders: these are quite expensive but they do give ideal presentation. Choose the braided leader that's exactly right for the job in hand. Some of them, for example, sink extremely quickly, whereas others will sit beautifully in the surface film. Most give an exceptionally good cast turnover. While on the subject of leaders, you might consider investing in some tippet rings. These are tiny silver rings that allow you to put droppers on your leader without the need for blood knots.

Fly lines are expensive and they need looking after. It makes sense, therefore, to buy some fly line treatments, which come in various types of dressings. Whenever you feel your casting is being held back a little, probably because of dirt and grit on the line, then it makes immediate sense to clean it thoroughly. Your casting will improve and the life of the line will be extended.

It's often important to keep dry flies in perfect, perky position on the surface film. Sprays and powders are good, but don't neglect physical fly dryers like Amadou or other water-absorbent materials. I've already mentioned fly boxes. Go for the very best—your flies need to be safe, secure, and away from damp. Make sure the fastening is tight. There's nothing more annoying than seeing your flies scattered through your tackle bag or, worse, along the bank.

➢ COMPACT

Here you see an angler out in mid-river fishing intently, happy in the knowledge that all the tackle he's ever going to need for the situation is safely stowed in his vest. He's fishing a small, clear, comparatively heavily pressured chalk stream and it's on waters like this that presentation has to be absolutely perfect. If the fly is going to float then it needs to do so beautifully. If it's going to sink, then you've got to get it down fast.

Zingers are important. These are simply small, retractable reels that you pin to your jacket and on which you can hang scissors, clippers, forceps, or whatever you are likely to need immediately to hand. Clippers are especially important. They provide a quick, simple way to trim all knots and they often incorporate a piercing tool that can clear the varnish from the eye of a fly. I particularly like to see a Ketchum release on a zinger. This is a little gadget that releases fish and avoids all fish handling. You simply run the Ketchum release down the leader and over the fly. The hook backs out with minimum damage to the fish.

A thermometer is infinitely useful, as you'll often gain fascinating insights into how a water works by knowing the exact temperature throughout the day. Just the rise or fall of a degree or two can spark all manner of changes in fly life and how the trout feed. If you're also going to be deeply concerned with

◄ WADING IN SAFETY

The wading staff is a vital third leg if you're thinking of wading water that's quick or deep or unknown to you. Mind you, don't let the added security of a wading staff lead you into situations you could possibly come to regret. Always regard water as potentially dangerous and never take risks. It's also important to tie a belt around your chest waders so that if you do fall they don't flood. Don't make a potentially fatal mistake like this particular angler.

the biology of fishing, then a marrow scoop is a good idea. With this you can check the stomach contents of any fish you decide to kill for the table. Knowing what the fish has recently fed on can provide invaluable clues to the fly you need on your leader.

If you're doing any serious wading, I'd certainly recommend a wading staff. These really do give an amazing amount of extra support in a heavy current or if you're moving over an unstable bottom. A wading

staff retractor is also vital, so that when you reach your fishing point you can begin to cast unhampered but still have the staff readily and safely to hand. If you are going to do much wading, you should also consider purchasing a life preserver.

When it comes to safety, you are going to need a small flashlight for fishing at dusk or at night, for sea trout perhaps. Don't overuse it because you'll kill your night vision. But, of course, it's invaluable for re-tying flies, for example.

Clothing

What you wear is vitally important: if you are cold or wet you simply won't concentrate and you'll probably want to pack up early. Make sure that your fishing coat, therefore, is up to the job. Chest waders are a good purchase—they're essential if you're going to be wading, but they also keep the elements out even if you're sitting in a boat. If you know you are never going to wade, gumboots and waterproof leggings will do the job, but make sure the quality is of the highest. Gore-Tex and similar materials really have taken over from old-style waxed cotton. They are breathable, light, and totally waterproof. I would always choose Gore-Tex waders rather than neoprene: they are brilliant for warm weather, and in winter you simply wear them over fleece leggings. A hat is useful for protecting the ears from a wayward fly, and a broad brim cuts down on light and helps the work of your glasses.

The color of your clothing is also an interesting question. Traditionally, we fisher folk wear dark greens and olives, presumably to merge in seamlessly with forest or moorland. From my diving experiences I'm not sure that's exactly how the fish see us from below, and if you're contemplating a really rugged wilderness expedition then perhaps garments a little bit more colorful could help in an emergency situation when you need to be spotted quickly.

This may all sound incredibly complex, but it isn't really. Take your time and keep your head when choosing tackle. Think where the bulk of your fishing is going to take place and ask for advice. Don't become obsessed by tackle—decide what you want, choose with care, buy the best you can afford, and get on with the job of fishing.

⋏ SHAD TIME

There is a period in the spring when the shad run some river systems in vast numbers. These are herring-like creatures, up to 5–6 pounds and their fight is quite extraordinary. Shad will take any gaudy fly.

➤ ON TOP OF THE WORLD

This is the beauty of fly fishing. Choose your clothing, your waders, and your tackle carefully, and you're free to roam far and wide into the most remote hinterlands to find vast extents of water. Remember, the further you get off the beaten track the more fish you are likely to find and the less wary they are likely to be. Two hours spent walking can truly pay dividends and take you to places that are absolutely spellbinding.

FOOD, FEEDING, AND FLIES

A GREAT BOOM IN THE ENTOMOLOGY OF FLY FISHING, THE STUDY OF THE INSECT SPECIES THAT INTEREST THE FLY ANGLER, BEGAN AROUND THE MIDDLE OF THE 19TH CENTURY, AND THERE'S BEEN A GROWING FOCUS ON THE IMITATIVE PROPERTIES OF NEW FLY PATTERNS EVER SINCE. OF COURSE, TO IMITATE THE FISH'S FOOD YOU'VE GOT TO BE ABLE TO IDENTIFY IT AND RECOGNIZE IT FIRST.

To help in this complex identification task there have been many scientific tomes published on the subject. These can make for heavy reading, so I'm going to miss out the Latin-quoting, professorial approach and try to get you down to the waterside where, really, everything begins and ends.

Beneath the Surface

So, you're standing there, fly rod in hand, tackle in your bag or your vest, looking at a river or a stillwater—and nothing, simply nothing, is rising. What is going on? Surely the fish need to feed? Well, a vast percentage of what fish eat lives down deep amid the security of stones and weed on the bed. The creatures we're talking about include freshwater shrimp, beetles, water fleas, tadpoles, water boatmen, snails of all sorts, and, of course, a huge

➢ MAN AND NATURE

When you're fishing tiny, crystal streams such as this, it's desperately important to creep up on the fish to watch exactly what they're feeding on and how they are behaving. This is the true art of fly fishing, and you're getting close to the supreme challenge here. Big, wild, wary fish are hugely satisfying to deceive. You'll know you've deciphered all the riddles of the fly-fisher's world when you reach this level of success.

A FLY-FISHER'S SELECTION

1   **STREAMER FLY** *A large streamer fly is useful for big trout, steelhead, muskie or pike—anything that wants a large meal.*

2   **WOOLY BUGGERS** *A lure such as this is excellent for trout.*

3   **WET FLIES** *Traditional wet flies are best fished on quick rivers for trout and grayling.*

4   **SALMON FLY** *This is a good example of a fly that will attract salmon.*

5   **DRY FLIES** *These are perfect for the summer and autumn trout river.*

6   **NYMPHS** *Nymphs are the standard patterns for deeper-feeding trout and grayling, and for many non-game fish.*

number of nymphs. The nymphs will eventually ascend to the surface, shed their skins, and transform into fully-matured flies, and trout love to feed on them as they're rising and hatching, as well as on the flies into which they turn.

A lot of the trout's food under the surface comes to them along with the drift of the current. Trout position themselves so they can see clearly what the river is bringing to them. The best lies offer the best views and these are generally taken by the biggest, most aggressive fish. The drift of food isn't constant throughout the day—it increases, obviously, when fly life is particularly active. It also reaches its height during the hours of darkness, when many aquatic creatures believe it's safe to move. Take time out to watch how natural prey behaves in the current. It's vital that your own lures copy natural prey as accurately as possible.

Fish, trout especially, don't always rely just on the drift for their food. Sometimes they'll adopt a more workaday, hands-on approach and actually dig for nymphs in weed or among stones. Bass will hunt small crayfish, and you'll find bonefish chasing crabs. So, whatever you're fishing for, it often pays to put an imitative pattern right down there on the bottom and work it slowly and tightly. Often, takes will be powerful and unmissable, but frequently you'll just notice a slight tightening or slackening of the line. Strike the moment your suspicions are aroused.

If you adopt this careful, imitative approach, don't be in a hurry to move on. It's likely that you're fishing the nymph in a subtle, difficult-to-spot fashion, and you could make several casts and work an area thoroughly before your fly is spotted.

Try a Nymph

So, it doesn't matter that nothing is rising, because now you can try your first choice, which is to fish a nymph deep and retrieve it slowly and thoughtfully.

Don't be too confused by the welter of nymph patterns available—there are simply hundreds. The key is to choose flies that blend in with the surroundings—hence brown, green, and black are generally successful—and move them back in a slow and lifelike way.

My favorite nymphs would probably include Pheasant Tails, Montanas, mayfly nymphs, various olives, and black spiders. I'd fish one or two of these patterns hard before

giving up on them. Experiment with various depths if necessary, putting on an intermediate or sinking line if you suspect that the fish are down deep because of cold or extreme heat.

There's no magic fly, but there are expert ways of working them. Think how you can impart life and realistic movement. It's a good idea to buy yourself an aquarium—it needn't be very large—and install all manner of aquatic life in it. Spend time just watching how nymphs and underwater insects move—carefully, cautiously, in short erratic bursts. It's these movements you're trying to imitate when you retrieve your fly through the water.

◄ CADDIS LARVA

Virtually all fish species, not just trout and grayling, feed heavily on caddis. These little grubs, which will eventually hatch out into glorious flies, generally form protective cases around themselves of either grains of sand, flakes of gravel, or pieces of weed.

➤ THE ADULT SEDGE

Caddis will then change into the pupa form, which ascends quickly to the surface and hatches out into the adult fly. Here we have the glorious sedge. There are all manner of sedges and they form an important part of the fish's diet through the warmer months of the year. You'll see sedges causing a disturbance on the surface of the water as they scuttle for cover.

◄ NYMPHS

If you take a sample of stones or weed from the gravel, the chances are, if it's a fertile water, you'll find scores and scores of nymphs that will live there between six months and two years depending on the species. Eventually, they'll leave the water and hatch, and at this stage they become very active and particularly vulnerable to predators.

Imitative Alternatives

If your nymph patterns resolutely refuse to work, you can try imitating the other food sources that I've already mentioned. Try various shrimp patterns in pink or green, or an ant or beetle imitation, best used on a floating line with a long leader.

Still nothing doing? Now is the time to use a fish or fry imitation. The idea here is to strip a fish imitation back quickly, and takes now will be aggressive and hard-hitting. This is an effective way of exploring large areas of water on bigger lakes, where location is a problem. Try flies such as the Muddler Minnow, wooly buggers, leech patterns, zonkers, and sculpin imitations.

Let's suppose that you're beginning to see movements just beneath the surface, often resulting in a boil displacing water. If there's a ripple on, you might suddenly notice flat, calm spots amid the chop. These are caused by trout coming up towards the surface and intercepting nymphs as they rise from the bottom to hatch out. This

⋏ DECISION TIME
Even a stocked rainbow will approach a fly with caution, particularly if it's been pricked or seen a fellow shoal member make a mistake and be caught. Obviously, there are times that fish fling themselves at anything even remotely edible, but it's a mistake to think this happens all the time. Regard every fish as difficult, and never underestimate your opponent.

⋎ LOOKING UP
What a trout sees and what it makes of what it sees we're never going to know exactly, but it is instructive to see how unlike the real insect our own artificials inevitably are. One of the major problems always, it seems to me, is the hook itself. A silver hook, so much the norm, frequently catches the light and reflects it in a most unnatural fashion, giving off a warning to the trout.

➤ DUNS AND SPINNERS
The nymphs finally rise to the surface, where they are trapped in the surface film until the wing case splits open and out climbs the winged fly. It's now called a dun, and it remains on the surface of the water until its wings are dry. This dun stage can last for just a few minutes or up to several days in the case of mayflies. It will then be transformed again by shedding the skin to become a spinner. Now the fly is ready to mate.

⋖ THE SHRIMP
Freshwater shrimp are found both in still and running water, and they are heavily preyed upon. Look for them in shallow, stony, weedy areas. You'll find they're a particularly important food source during the colder months of the season when there's not much fly life about.

is the time to make sure that you're fishing a floating line and letting your nymph patterns sink just a foot or so beneath the surface. Move them back slowly towards you. Don't rush, and be ready for subtle takes.

⋎ QUITE A MOUTHFUL
OK, this streamer doesn't look like much out of the water, but below the surface its movements are mighty reminiscent of a small, fleeing fish out of its depth in the main flow of the river—an easy target for a hungry predator.

⋏ AN IMITATION OF LIFE
Larger flies, streamers, big lures, and salmon flies might not imitate anything exactly but they do give an impression of movement and fluidity, and of a ready meal. In short, anything that looks alive and is of edible size is frequently going to be investigated.

Quite a Buzz

Better still, you are now seeing what we call head and tail rises—actually watching the fish move through the surface film. Sometimes you'll see the head followed by the curve of the back. The dorsal fin will frequently be held clear, and sometimes the tip of the tail fin, before the fish goes down. Almost certainly these fish are taking midges, and midge fishing is as exciting as it gets.

Midges are small chironimid larvae that begin life as bloodworms in the silt and mud of the bed. These eventually turn into pupae, which rise to the surface and hatch out in to the adult nymph. As the pupa— the midge—struggles in the surface film to slough its skin, it's incredibly tempting to the trout. The hatches are prolific, and it can seem that every fish in the lake is feeding in the surface film.

Standard patterns have worked well for years, but the new shiny epoxy midges are proving dramatically effective. Fish all midge patterns on a floating line so that you can work them either in the surface film or just an inch or two beneath. Let them hang motionless, or twitch them slowly back toward you. Watch the path of individual feeding fish and place your midge where you predict it's about to arrive.

Other flies make easy targets in and around the surface film as they emerge, so if your midge patterns aren't working, or if you see larger flies in the air, try alternative patterns. The Hoppers are excellent, as are Hares Ears, and the various Emerger patterns that are often tied with a little polystyrene ball to keep them hanging in the crucial zone. Fishing the surface film is one of the most productive forms of fly fishing.

THE ADULT MIDGE

The adult flies often sit on the water for a while and are vulnerable to the fish. So, too, are the females when they return to the water's surface to lay their eggs. The adults can be imitated as well as the pupa. Try small Griffith's gnats, for example.

THE HATCHING MIDGE

Escaping the pupal case can be a drawn-out process, and the hatching midge is very vulnerable to preying trout. The cast-off skins are sticky, and when there is a great deal of hatching activity you'll sometimes find them clinging to your fly line when you retrieve it.

THE LARVA

The larvae of the midge are commonly called bloodworms, and they can be anywhere up to an inch long. You'll find them in the mud of the river or lake bed or among bottom vegetation. At this stage they're of little use to the fly fisherman, although non-game fish feed on them heavily, blowing up the bottom to get at the tasty morsels.

THE PUPA

Midges hatch generally from early spring onward. At first, you'll find them hatching in the day, but as the season progresses they become more active toward evening. The pupae rise through the water but have quite a problem getting through the surface film. They hang there very exposed in the top layer before hatching, and it's at this time you'll see the distinctive, bulging rise forms.

⋏ FLAT-WINGED FLIES

There are thousands of species of flat-winged flies, for example, houseflies, mosquitoes, and crane flies. They're characterized by their six legs and their two flat, short wings. Many are land insects, but there are several hundred aquatic species as well. Midges are among the most important for the fisherman. Midge fishing can be useful in almost any month of the year.

The life cycle of the midge is egg to larva to pupa to adult. Remember all these can take on a wide range of colors. For example, the larvae can be red, grey, or black with virtually any shade in between. Pupae can be orange or black and they can even change color. The adults, too, can be many various shades. For this reason, it's a good idea to have different colored midges in your box. Red and black are the usual favorites, but don't neglect olives, yellows, and different shades of green.

It's probable that on many waters buzzers make up the principal food source of the trout population, so don't overlook them.

THE SPINNER

The dun then molts again and becomes the shining adult, known to scientists as the imago but to anglers as the spinner. Spinners swarm over the water during May and June, unable to feed because their mouths have degenerated. Mating takes place in flight and the male dies, falls to the surface, and is eaten by birds or fish. The female lays her eggs on the water's surface and is now "spent". Once again, the body presents a tasty meal for a fish.

THE DUN

At the surface the wing case of the nymph splits open and the winged fly emerges. It's now called a dun and it is forced to remain on the surface film until its wings are dry enough for it to fly. This can take minutes or up to 30 hours, depending on the species of the fly and the weather. Again, the dun is now very vulnerable to trout attack!

THE HATCHING NYMPH

When the nymphs are preparing to hatch they become very restless and often make test runs to the surface and back to the bottom again, an activity that leaves them very vulnerable. Eventually, however, they will rise to the surface for the final time and there they will begin to shed their skin.

THE NYMPH

The nymph of the upwinged fly lives among stones and bottom weeds. There are many different sorts of nymph—for example, there are 40 species of mayfly alone. Nymphs vary in size, but they're all eagerly taken by trout, especially when they move around looking for hiding places.

Moving to the Dry Fly

Let's say that you now see something altogether more dramatic—a splashing, noisy rise with the trout sometimes leaping clear of the surface altogether. This means that fish are chasing flies that are about to move from the surface and escape. A major hatch is on the boil and this is real guzzle time. You can still fish your nymph or emerger with success, but it's now that you can move on to the most exciting kind of fly fishing of all—the dry fly. However, to pick the right one you've got to look carefully at the insects in the air around you.

The Mayfly

Perhaps the most obvious of all dry flies are the mayflies that are seen on both rivers and lakes from late spring. These are large, beautiful, upwinged flies, which means that their wings stand proud and look like sails. Mayflies begin their lives down deep, as nymphs, and then ascend to the surface where they hatch into a dull, rather drab dun. These then dry, often in the margins of the river or lake, and transform once more into the fully formed spinner, which mates, lays eggs, and then dies. You can't miss mayflies—they are so large, so iridescent, and, frequently, so amazingly numerous. The air can seem full of them. The windshield of your car can be literally coated in the bodies of the spinners as they die. There are endless mayfly patterns— the Green Drake and Hendricksons are favorites. Take a variety of sizes and colors with you and try to match your artificial with the insects you see in the air or on the surface.

⋏ UPWINGED FLIES

Upwinged flies belong to the family ephemeroptera. There are many different types of insect in the group, but, big or small, they all have sail-like wings and either two or three long tails. Olives and mayflies are the two most important members of the family as far as fishermen are concerned, and the mayfly is particularly dramatic. These truly are beautiful insects when mature, and they illuminate rivers and lakes generally from around mid-May to early June. The mayfly season is very short and the adult insects live for only a few hours or days, during which time mating and egg laying are their sole purposes.

⋏ SPENT FLIES
Cautious trout look for flies as they lie dying in eddies; let an artificial become bogged down in the surface film and twitch it if a fish passes by.

The Olive

Throughout the summer and into the autumn you'll frequently see flies looking like the mayfly but only a half or a third as large. These belong to the abundant olive family. Once again, try to match your imitation with the hatch and copy closely the size and color of the natural. Olive duns are favorite, along with iron-blue duns and large dark olives. Make sure you have blue-winged olives with you.

The Sedge

Perhaps the flies in the air are sedges. Their larvae (commonly called caddis grubs) build protective cocoons from gravel, sticks, sand, or shells, in which they shelter on the bed of the river or lake. The caddis nymphs eventually come to the surface and hatch out looking like reddish-brown moths with two large, forward-pointing antennae. You'll find most sedge hatching out in the afternoons and evenings, and you'll recognize them by their large, rooflike wings, as well as by those antennae. Artificials such as the Goddard and Elk Hair imitate sedges.

The Damsel and Others

You certainly won't miss a hatch of damselflies, those beautiful creatures with their distinctive electric-blue bodies and wide wingspan. Damselfly nymphs are often more popular with the fish, but the dry damsel pattern is always worth a go. Don't strike too soon at a rise, because trout will often drown the fly before eventually taking it in. Once you've seen the rise, count slowly to three or four before tightening.

Also be aware of what are known as terrestrials—flies that are blown onto the water from the surrounding bankside. These include ants, beetles, grasshoppers, and crickets. Many will be blown into the water on a breeze and feeding can be frenetic.

As the summer progresses, you will find more and more crane flies blown onto the surface of both rivers and lakes. These are incredibly popular with fish. They are big, prolific, and relatively easy for the fish to catch. In areas where the hatches of sedges and olives seem to be diminishing, crane flies are increasingly targeted. Don't worry if you don't see any fish feeding on the surface. The crane fly is so big and so desirable

that your imitation will often pull them up from many feet down.

In a Nutshell

So what are the keys to all this? Firstly, you've got to look at the water carefully. If there's no movement, fish deep. If there is movement just beneath the surface or in the surface film, that's where you've got to fish. If you actually see the full-blooded rise, this is the time to get your dry flies out. Observe what is lifting off the water, decide what manner of fly it is, and do your best to imitate it as closely as possible.

This is a rough guide, but its aim is to convince you to use your eyes, have patience, and begin to build up a knowledge that will be both satisfying and highly productive.

⋎ THE ATTACK
A fly is taken with great gusto by a bass, and the bottom silt is lifted by the force of the fish bellying.

SKILLS

SMOOTH, ACCURATE, CONSISTENT CASTING IS CLEARLY ONE OF THE PRIME SKILLS NEEDED IN FLY FISHING. ALTHOUGH I'VE WRITTEN ABOUT FLY CASTING ON MANY OCCASIONS AND I'VE TAUGHT HUNDREDS OF ANGLERS TO PUT OUT A REASONABLY DECENT LINE, I'M INDEBTED IN THIS CHAPTER TO MICHAEL EVANS, A GREAT FRIEND AND A FULL-TIME PROFESSIONAL FLY-FISHING INSTRUCTOR, FOR HIS ADVICE.

Watching Michael perform is a revelation. It's hard to put into words exactly what makes Michael so superior, so poised, and so supremely good to watch. Part of the mixture is certainly athleticism—his footing and how he shapes his body. There is a certain amount of power involved, true, but most of the energy comes not from brute force but from timing and technique. Michael can make a line arrow out like few others, and he obviously takes a very physical pleasure in putting out a perfect cast. In Michael's hands, casting becomes a goal and an objective in itself. Fishing, or at least the catching of fish, is a secondary consideration altogether. It's almost like clay-pigeon shooting in a way—there doesn't have to be a flesh and blood product at the end of the day to make a field sport well worthwhile.

Basic Fly Casting

The first principle to take on board is that the rod must do the work, not you! Hold the rod and pretend that you want to flick a piece of mud off the tip. The flex of the rod is the action you want, not a gradual pushing movement. The line has to follow the path the rod top takes and the top of your rod follows the path of your thumb. The rod merely amplifies the movement of your hand, so always watch your thumb when correcting faults.

The first hurdle, and the hardest thing you will ever do, is to learn to get the line out. As your experience builds up, you will learn to false cast and shoot line but, for now, if you're starting on water, you must make do with first pulling 2 or 3 yards of line, plus your leader, out of the tip ring of the rod and dropping it onto the

➤ SPEED AND ACCURACY

OK, there are no snags around if you're bone fishing on the Flats, but what Roger has to contend with here, apart from sneaky breezes, is the problem of fast-moving fish that demand complete accuracy. When his guide points to a shoal then Roger has to place his fly with pinpoint precision in a matter of seconds. There's no time here for false casting, which would alarm the fish anyway. It's a matter of lift, push, and trust in your own skill.

◄ STEALTH

Remember that it's not always a case of simply standing on the bankside and flexing a traditional overhead cast. Many times you're going to be called upon to cast from a kneeling position, from behind trees, into strong headwinds, or in any one of a hundred conditions that defy the textbooks.

water in front of you. Then, by wiggling the rod tip from side to side, you can drag more out through the rod tip as you pull it off the reel. You need about 10 yards of free line in all, which by now will look like a plate of spaghetti on the water in front of you. Don't panic. This is what you want.

The Roll Cast

Now you need to learn the basic roll cast before any other, because however strong the urge may be to go straight to the overhead cast, which is the main one in the trout-fisher's armory, you must not attempt to overhead cast a badly crooked line off the water.

The roll cast, therefore, is the first essential, as you can use it to straighten an untidy line before moving to an overhead cast. It also has other uses. You can use it as a cast in its own right when you have

no room for a back cast, you can use it for safety when casting from a boat in a high wind, and you can use it to get a sunk line out of the water.

The basic movements of the roll cast are lift, sweep, and hit. The lift starts with the rod tip touching the water. You then lift it slowly but smoothly up to the 11 o'clock position (12 o'clock would be vertical) and pause. This should bring the line nearest the rod top off the water with the rest feathering along the surface toward you.

Now we move to the sweep. Presuming you're casting with the right hand, swing the rod tip out to the right of you and sweep smoothly back in a wide arc around and up until your thumb is level with your right ear and the rod is pointing back to 2 o'clock. Pause again. At this point your wrist should have cocked back and the position of the rod should allow a loop of line to

form behind your shoulder, curving down to the water beside you and looking much like the letter D.

Now for the hit. Remember the flicking movement we discussed at the beginning. Drive your thumb forward in a flicking movement as if you were swatting a fly on the wall just in front of you. If you are using the roll, aim straight at the target; cast to reach a fish; and stop sharply again at 10 o'clock in front of you. This should literally flick the line off the water and roll it through the air toward the target. The line should land in a straight line out in front.

▼ THE BASIC ROLL CAST

The roll cast straightens an untidy line before you move into an overhead cast. It's also a really important cast in its own right, especially on small rivers or when there's no room to back cast because of tree cover. You can also use it for safety, especially in a boat when the weather is very windy. It's also the ideal cast to lift a sunken line out of the water.

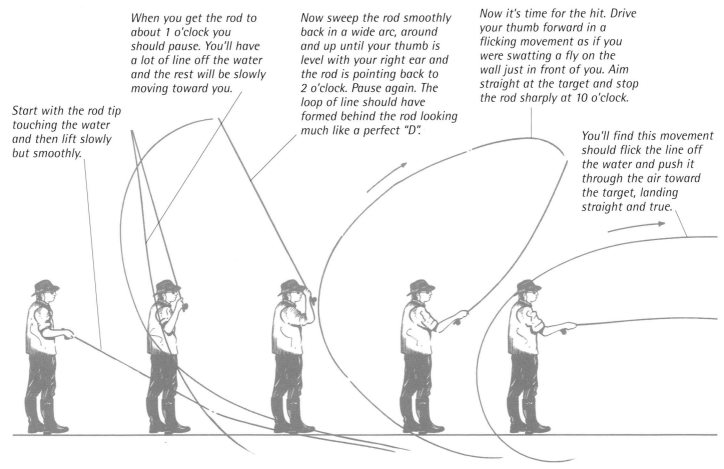

Start with the rod tip touching the water and then lift slowly but smoothly.

When you get the rod to about 1 o'clock you should pause. You'll have a lot of line off the water and the rest will be slowly moving toward you.

Now sweep the rod smoothly back in a wide arc, around and up until your thumb is level with your right ear and the rod is pointing back to 2 o'clock. Pause again. The loop of line should have formed behind the rod looking much like a perfect "D".

Now it's time for the hit. Drive your thumb forward in a flicking movement as if you were swatting a fly on the wall just in front of you. Aim straight at the target and stop the rod sharply at 10 o'clock.

You'll find this movement should flick the line off the water and push it through the air toward the target, landing straight and true.

The Overhead Cast

As I have said, this is the main cast in the trout-fisher's armory, and you must learn it before going fishing. The roll cast will get about 10 yards of line out straight in front of you, and this means that you've got enough line to play with to learn the overhead cast properly.

The overhead cast is essentially made up of three basic movements—a lift, a back cast, and a forward cast. Every cast you make depends upon the success of all three stages, and the key positions you should look for at each stage can be best summarized in three words. Tip. Top. Ten. Let's run through them.

▼ THE OVERHEAD CAST
This is the main cast in the fly-fisher's armory and you must learn it before going on to other techniques. It's simple and there are only three basic movements—the lift, the back cast, and the forward cast—so don't be intimidated.

Your thumb should now be level with your right eye with the rod pointing at about the 12 o'clock position. The inertia of the rod will have allowed it to go further back to about 1 o'clock. Don't let the rod go back further than this or the cast will fail.

Start with the rod tip just touching the water and the line straight out.

Lift slightly with the forearm and accelerate gently.

You are now casting forward with your thumb driving the rod down. Stop at the 10 o'clock position in front of you. This movement feels like a tap with a small hammer or swatting a fly against a wall.

The line is now flying out in front of you, arrowing to its desired position.

Tip

Start with the rod tip touching the water and the line straight out in front of you. Lift slightly with the forearm and accelerate back and up with the rod as if moving the thumb up an imaginary escalator toward a position level with your right eye. If you assume that you started at an imaginary clock position of, say, 8 o'clock, you will be accelerating through 9, 10, and 11 o'clock, and just as you get past 11 o'clock you need to add a short flick of the wrist before stopping sharply with your thumb pointing straight up to the top. This is called the back cast, but it would be better called the up cast.

Top

With your thumb level with your right eye and pointing straight up at 12 o'clock, the momentum of the rod will have allowed it to go slightly further, say to 1 o'clock. It must not be allowed to go further than this or the cast will fail. To check that you are doing this right, make sure that the butt of the rod doesn't move more than 2 or 3 inches away from your forearm. If you did this correctly, the line will have flicked back and up into the air behind you, and it needs a short pause in which to straighten before you start the forward cast.

Ten

For the forward cast, press firmly onward again with your thumb sliding back down the escalator before stopping sharply at the 10 o'clock position in front of you. This movement should feel rather like a tap with a small hammer and should flick the line out across and above the water before settling. The sharp stop to the forward movement of the rod is crucial, as without this your leader is likely to crumple down onto the water in a pile of loops. That's all there is to it, but the timing is everything.

Additional Tips

Once you've learned the overhead cast, you can consider elaborations such as the single and double hauls. These are primarily to get distance or to increase line speed to combat wind. Hauling is a technique where the non-casting hand tugs at the spare line being held between the butt ring and reel to increase the momentum and therefore the loading of the rod spring on the forward and/or back cast.

When casting, always grip the rod handle very gently with the thumb on top of the cork as if you were shaking hands with it.

If you are right-handed, you will make fewer mistakes if you start with the right foot slightly forward.

If you're having trouble with your overhead casting, the cause may very well be what instructors call breaking the wrist, that is allowing your wrist to cock back at the top of your cast. To correct this fault, try tucking the butt of the rod inside your coat cuff. Although it feels awkward, this prevents the rod from breaking too far back and will improve your casting.

Curved and slack line casts are designed to create "mends" or to put slack into the line on the water to overcome drag, and they're normally only necessary when using a dry fly on rivers. The secret is to make sure you don't make any of the additional movements until after the power has been put into the line on the forward cast and the rod has reached the 10 o'clock forward position.

➢ MENDING THE LINE

Ken Whelan, that doyen of Irish fly fishermen, has put out a comparatively light line on a small river for summer grilse. Notice now how he's flicking the rod tip in a left-to-right circular movement so that the line is lifted and looped back across the current. This will give him valuable seconds during which time the line will not be affected by the current and the fly will not, therefore, be pulled unnaturally off its true course. Successful fly fishing is as much a matter of mental effort as physical prowess.

➢ A MASTER AT WORK

Michael Evans is pictured here demonstrating his mastery of the Spey cast. If you ask Michael what the secret is to his casting success it would probably boil down to the two "T"s – Timing and Technique. Everything that Michael does looks totally unhurried, unflustered, and completely controlled. This is partly innate ability but, like any champion caster, Michael practices extensively.

THE DOUBLE HAUL

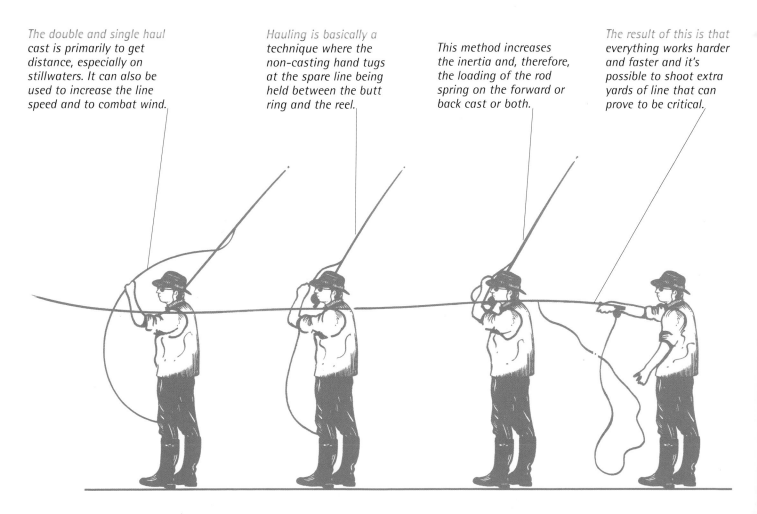

The double and single haul cast is primarily to get distance, especially on stillwaters. It can also be used to increase the line speed and to combat wind.

Hauling is basically a technique where the non-casting hand tugs at the spare line being held between the butt ring and the reel.

This method increases the inertia and, therefore, the loading of the rod spring on the forward or back cast or both.

The result of this is that everything works harder and faster and it's possible to shoot extra yards of line that can prove to be critical.

◄ THE PERFECT BACK CAST

There's a lot to be seen in this sequence of photographs. Firstly, notice how Don has waded out into the river but is still pressed tight against the rushes, which break up his outline. Now look at that perfect back cast, stopped resolutely at the 1 o'clock position. The line has straightened out nicely behind him and he is ready to make the forward cast.

⌄ OUT IT GOES

And again, Don is fishing classically. Now his rod stops at the 10 o'clock position. The rod tip is a blur, working incredibly quickly, flicking the line upriver to the waiting trout. Notice the minimal amount of effort. Note, too, that not a ripple is given off by his body, which remains perfectly still. Casting comes naturally—his entire attention is focused on the fish and presentation of the fly.

The Spey Cast

Let's now look at salmon fishing and the Spey cast. There's no magic about a Spey cast, and in simple terms it's merely a speeded up roll cast, which you can now already do. Spey casts have several advantages over the overhead cast. They are more efficient for wide-angle direction changes. They can be carried out in places with little or no room for a back cast. They are also a lot safer because the fly never goes behind the caster. You only need to be clouted in the back of the head once by a 2-inch brass tube traveling at full speed to understand the benefits. Although it is almost impossible to learn the Spey cast from a book, let me attempt to explain the principles. Let's concentrate on the single Spey and the double Spey. The choice of which to use depends solely upon the wind direction.

With an upstream wind, the single Spey is used because the fly and loop are swept upstream before hitting out to the target. If it's a downstream wind, you'll need the double Spey cast where the fly and loop are kept downstream prior to hitting out to the target.

Which bank you are on will dictate which hand is uppermost on the rod. You will need to be able to cast in either direction, and it's no more difficult to cast from either shoulder as long as you remember to use equal force from both hands.

◄ THE CRITICAL MOMENT

Casting the fly is little more than a mechanical process and the real skill begins now that the fly is in the water, drifting back down with the current. Don has to watch its course minutely and be as close to 100 percent certain as he can be when a take actually occurs. Notice how he's feeding back the line through his fingers, and his eyes, behind polarizing glasses, are intently focused.

▼ AND IT ALL COMES TOGETHER

Seeing the fish, getting into position, working out the strategy, putting out the fly, seeing and connecting with the take—these are the issues that have Don obsessed with the sport. OK, the fight is fun—especially this one, which took him down and across the river—but it's the intellectual game rather than the physical scrap that grabs most experienced fly fishermen.

The Single Spey

If you're fishing from the left bank, your right hand is up. If you're on the right bank, your left hand is up.

Stand facing square onto the target. Leave the rod pointing downstream at the fished-out line with the tip of the rod at the waterline. To do this, your hands will be rather awkwardly crossed with the rod across your stomach.

Now, to waltz time, LIFT. Raise the rod by bending your upper forearm at the elbow slightly toward the near bank. Aim for about 10 o'clock on your rod clock. Pause for the count of three and now move into the SWEEP. Turn right with your upper hand and sweep away out and around an imaginary plate sitting on your right shoulder until your right thumb comes around to the side of your right shoulder and up to a position level with your right ear. Pause again for the count of three. This movement should have swept the line and fly upstream so that at least 3 yards of line and the leader splash down approximately a rod-and-a-half's length away from you upstream. The "D" loop formed behind the rod is facing the target.

Now for the HIT. Punch the rod smartly forward, stopping sharply at 10 o'clock in front of you, flicking the loop of line out, across, and above the water. This is a wrist and forearm flick with both hands to flex the rod—it is not a shoulder heave.

The Double Spey

Now for the single Spey's big brother. On the left bank, your left hand is up; on the right bank, your right hand. The double Spey has just one extra movement to the single Spey, but the double Spey with a short line is easier than the single Spey because the timing is less critical.

If you are standing on the right bank with a good downstream wind, you must again face the target, but leave the rod pointing at the fished-out line downstream. With the rod across your stomach and your right hand uppermost, your hands will not be crossed.

Tow some line upstream. Lift just slightly and tow the rod top upstream until your hands are crossed over as they were for the single Spey. This will bring enough line upstream to form the loop, but will leave the fly still downstream of you. That's vital.

Now LIFT. As with the single Spey, lift up to the 10 o'clock position and slightly in toward the nearside bank upstream. Again, pause for the count of two and three.

Now SWEEP. As with the single Spey, sweep out, around (that is, back downstream) and lift back up to level with your right ear. As you do this, the line will peel back down and around before forming the "D" loop behind the rod just off your downstream shoulder. The foot of the loop and the fly and leader will be anchored in the water. Pause again for the count of three. Now HIT. Drive the loop out with the movement you learned with the single Spey.

After you've learned these two basic casts you'll be ready for the snake roll, which is probably best taught by an instructor. Only use a snake roll if there's a downstream wind, or it can be dangerous.

THE SINGLE SPEY

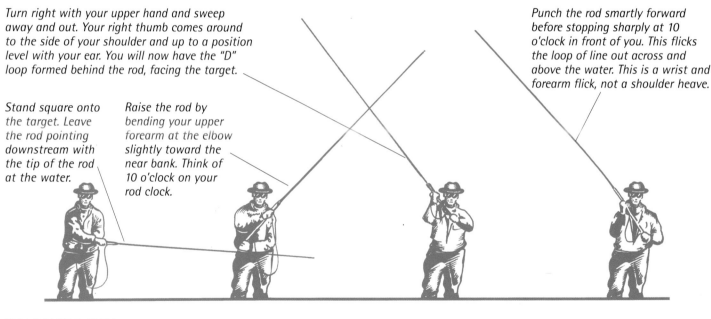

Stand square onto the target. Leave the rod pointing downstream with the tip of the rod at the water.

Raise the rod by bending your upper forearm at the elbow slightly toward the near bank. Think of 10 o'clock on your rod clock.

Turn right with your upper hand and sweep away and out. Your right thumb comes around to the side of your shoulder and up to a position level with your ear. You will now have the "D" loop formed behind the rod, facing the target.

Punch the rod smartly forward before stopping sharply at 10 o'clock in front of you. This flicks the loop of line out across and above the water. This is a wrist and forearm flick, not a shoulder heave.

THE DOUBLE SPEY

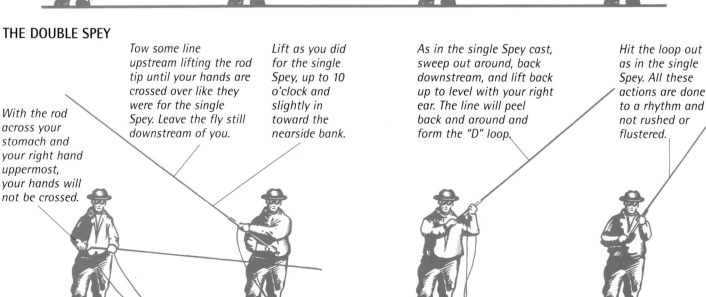

With the rod across your stomach and your right hand uppermost, your hands will not be crossed.

Tow some line upstream lifting the rod tip until your hands are crossed over like they were for the single Spey. Leave the fly still downstream of you.

Lift as you did for the single Spey, up to 10 o'clock and slightly in toward the nearside bank.

As in the single Spey cast, sweep out around, back downstream, and lift back up to level with your right ear. The line will peel back and around and form the "D" loop.

Hit the loop out as in the single Spey. All these actions are done to a rhythm and not rushed or flustered.

SAFETY CONSIDERATIONS

1 You will already have picked up throughout this book that I'm a firm believer in anglers wearing polarizing glasses at all times, because you can see so much more through the surface of the water. This is especially important when fly casting, as you want to target your fish as accurately as possible. They also help you to see the riverbed when wading, and may prevent you stepping into a deep hole!

2 The eye protection that glasses offer is vital, too. Remember you have a hooked artificial fly traveling around your head and body all day long, frequently at great speeds. There is that ever-distinct possibility that a gust of wind could blow it directly at your face. I've seen people with hooks in their noses and ears, and I've had one in my scalp. That's bad enough, but the thought of a hook in the eye... Wear those glasses.

3 To avoid hooking yourself, always check wind speed and direction. Be very wary of a wind that is blowing the fly line actually toward you. If you're right-handed, this obviously means a wind coming from the right. Try to avoid such a situation, especially when you're a beginner.

4 Once again, as in nearly all forms of fishing, use a barbless hook or flatten the barb when you're fly fishing. Should anything go wrong, a barbless hook slips out with relatively little pain or fuss.

5 Always check above and behind you for any power lines. Remember how easily electricity is conducted through carbon.

6 When you are fly fishing, always be aware of anybody moving behind you along the bank. Never risk that quick cast before they arrive, just in case you get your timing wrong.

7 Whenever you move position it's a good idea to look behind you to see if there are any problematic trees or bushes... or livestock! I've actually seen a young bull get hooked in the ear and run off all the line and backing!

8 If you're wading on a river or still water, it's frequently tempting to go out just that little bit further and deeper to reach rising fish. Do this very, very carefully, and always make sure that you're well within your depth. If you are wading, it's a good idea to have a wading stick with you to act as a third leg for balance and to be able to test depths in front. Be extra careful if there is a rapid current.

Additional Physical Skills

Casting sounds difficult, and it can look difficult, but it's not a magician's art. Try it on your own at first, but do get professional advice after a while to iron out any faults that you may be building into your action.

Casting, however, isn't the only physical skill to be used in fly fishing. General physical fitness can be very useful if you're fishing wild streams and you want to walk a fair way. Acute eyesight is really important, too. You should be able to recognize hatching insects, and it's essential that you're able to see your small, floating dry fly in low light conditions, so if your naked eye isn't up to it, get spectacles!

Hand-to-eye co-ordination is also an important part of the fly-fishing game. You need to time so many things in fly fishing—all aspects of the cast, as well as actually striking the fish when you have a take. Playing a big fish is also a skill that you will gradually learn. There's a good halfway house between bullying a fish and being too weak with it, and if you know the strength of your tackle and you're confident with it you can put a surprising amount of pressure on any fish. Don't let the fish dictate what goes on.

➢ IT CAN HAPPEN TO ANYONE
I'm not sure my subject will thank me for this particular photograph, but I think it's a valid one. Never, ever forget that all of us will foul up from time to time. It might be annoying, or amusing to others, but it's no disgrace. The angler who hasn't hooked a tree at some stage in his career just doesn't exist. Don't let the fear of a snag prevent you from fishing a difficult area, because it's often in exactly these places that the fish are most likely to be lying.

A Question of Attitude

When it comes to mental attitudes perhaps from the outset I should emphasize enjoyment. Don't be afraid of the seeming complexities of casting. Although there are over 30 casts to master, these shouldn't be regarded as intimidating but as pleasing challenges to meet head on. The same applies to fly recognition—you don't need a degree in natural history, just eyes, a textbook and some common sense. Fishing is fun, so keep it that way…

… which leads me immediately on to the philosophy of acceptance. Sometimes you'll succeed and sometimes you'll fail. If you fail, try calmly to work out why and accept blanks as part of the overall fun of the sport. Don't set yourself impossible targets and make a rod for your own back. Don't demand to be king of the river each and every day, because you'll be setting yourself up for endless disappointments. Learn to enjoy the successes of others around you just as much as your own. That way, every single fish that's caught will be a bonus, and your companions will rejoice for you, genuinely, when you have your great times.

None of us is fishing for survival, so you needn't be greedy for fish. Catch a fish or two by all means, but don't terrorize the water. If the fishery you are on is totally wild, then tread even more lightly along it. Wild fisheries are always lightly stocked, and they can be destroyed if anglers show a grasping attitude.

Take in everything that's happening around you on a fishing trip. This isn't pious nonsense, it's the true way to stay in the game for the rest of your life. Observe and appreciate wildlife—it can be absolutely spectacular, especially on

▾ ATHLETICISM

Fishing is about poise and grace, but there are times when you've really got to make your body work. Here, Charles Jardine is really straining to hit into a fish that has sipped in a nymph at some range. It's imperative that he tighten as quickly and as strongly as he can or the opportunity will be missed. It's a lightning quick, almost balletic movement, and he is rewarded with the solid thump of a hooked fish. Calm and cool a good fly fisherman should be… but not always!

> CRUCIAL MOMENT
A wild fish is always going to be more difficult to hoodwink than a stocked one. There's just something about them that makes them wary of their own shadows. This is the third time that this particular brown has inspected the fly. Perhaps it's the drag. Perhaps it's the pattern. Perhaps it's the size. There's just something ringing the caution bell and yet again it turns away, leaving the angler thoroughly frustrated.

our wilder waters. Speak to your guides. Listen to the murmur of the water over the shallows. Enjoy the freedom of the riverbank away from the office. Marvel at the beauty of the fish lying in the water beneath you.

Be bold and imaginative. Think of new techniques and new fly patterns… fly tying is a skill that I can't even begin to go into here, but it's an art form all its own, and one you might care to take up as your passion develops. Read widely, and I don't just mean the instructional stuff. There is an enormously rich literature of fly fishing that goes back decades, and it can be so rewarding if you delve deeply into it. Relish the passion of those who have gone before, and aspire to become not just a more successful fisherman but, in all ways, truly a better one.

PROBLEM BUSTING

Despite everything, your casting is not really progressing as you'd like. Let's have a look at some possible solutions.

1 Are you sure your rod and line are matched? It's no good using a heavy rod with a light line, or vice versa.

2 Is your back cast working properly? Are you letting it open out nicely behind you so that it's straight and level before you begin your forward cast? If you're letting that back cast droop and fall toward the ground, then you're in trouble.

3 Is the line traveling with enough speed? Don't be frightened of the whole process—attack the job with vim and vigor! Of course it is possible to overdo this, but it's better to err on the positive side than the negative.

4 It could be that your fly is simply too heavy to cast successfully. Very big lures do demand special casting techniques. It's far better to start off with a small nymph tied on a size 14 or 16 hook.

5 Are you trying to push your fly into too strong a wind? If there is much wind, it's easier to have the wind behind you. If it's blowing straight into your face, then even an expert will have problems. It is best to go out the first few times in conditions that are as calm as possible.

6 Is your leader too long? In certain specialized conditions, it's a good idea to have a long leader, but when you're beginning, don't tie one up that is longer than your rod. For example, if you're using a 9-foot rod, then an 8- or 9-foot leader is about right.

7 Are you being too ambitious, making too many false casts and trying to get out just a few too many yards of line? At first, style and technique are more important than distance. Providing your casting is tight and neat, it doesn't really matter if you are getting out 7 or 17 yards of line. It's better to concentrate on good short casting to start with rather than going for wild, long casts that are probably landing noisily and scaring fish away. You will find that your distance builds up gradually the more times you go out.

8 It could be that your fly line is sticky for some reason. Strip it off the reel and give it a good wash in warm, slightly soapy water. You'll be surprised at how much dirt and grit comes off. Once clean, you will find that your line slides much more easily through the rings.

Casting Skills From the Experts

I'm a decent caster, no more. I can get a fly out in most conditions with reasonable accuracy, but I must add there are many people much better than I. Many of them are my friends, and I have asked some of the better known and the more expert of them to pass on their own tips. Believe me, these are true words of wisdom.

• Bob Glynn—Mainstay of the North Wales Fly Fishing School

Begin your cast right at the bottom with the rod tip almost at the water itself. You'll find this loads the rod

⌄ IT'S ALL IN THE GRIP
This is a photograph of a fly-casting demonstration by expert angler Bob Glynn. Notice the straightness and rigidity of the wrist. Notice how the handle is held and how the rod is pointed at the exact target where Bob wants to land his fly. Most casting instructors would agree that it's important to keep the wrist rigid on the cast and not to let it break, especially when the back cast is taking place.

much more easily. Your back cast will be better and your forward casts much longer. Think about your stance, too, and the way your feet are positioned. Point your left foot to where you want to lay the cast down.

• Danny North—Sales Manager, Sportfish

My tip is to drift the rod. We're all taught that the rod movement should be between 10 o'clock and 1 o'clock, but this is old school and inflexible. Instead, drift the rod back to 1.30 or even 2 o'clock. You'll find that when the loop drifts behind you it opens up fully and gives you an extra 2 to 3 yards with the front cast.

This goes against everything you've ever been told, I know, but if you do drift it just these few extra inches, you'll find that extra leverage coming forward can make a huge difference.

• Charles Jardine

Practice. Pure and simple. I still practice each and every day, just like a professional golfer or tennis player. I work continuously at every element of my casting and realize that nothing drops into place without blood, sweat, and tears. It's totally unrealistic for a beginner to pick up a fly rod and think he's going to be world-class within a matter of hours. It doesn't matter how good you are, you can always be better.

• Hugh Falkus

In Spey casting the loop is absolutely everything, and you just can't get a cast out until your loops are perfect. Also, always try to keep your shoulders as still as possible. You can't Spey cast if you're jumping around like a marionette!

• Michael Evans

Always hold the handle of your rod as if it were very fragile. This lets the rod do the work and it will

improve your casting. If you're having trouble with your overhead casting it can very often be what instructors call "breaking the wrist". To correct this fault, try tucking the butt of the rod inside your sleeve.

• John Wolstenholme—Sportfish
You wouldn't think of taking up golf without a few lessons, and it's just the same with fishing. Get some proper lessons from properly accredited guys and you'll go a lot further a lot quicker. Don't be at all intimidated when you are with your instructor. Remember, instead, that he or she is there to help you in every way possible. If you have any questions, just ask. And even if

you're an accomplished fly fisher, it's not a bad idea to brush up on your casting skills from time to time.

• Gary Coxon—Representative of Sage rods in the UK and fly-fishing guru
It's important that people realize one rod will never do everything. Everyone tends to think that a 6-weight will do the lot, but it won't. You've got to pick the right rod for the right job ahead of you. Choose your rods carefully. I can't count the number of times I've seen people pick rods up, waggle them, and look down them to make sure the rings are straight. This is just about as useful as kicking car tires in a

showroom! You've got to try a rod out, if at all possible, before you actually go and buy the new one. Remember that some rods are just casting tools and are hopeless for fishing. What you want is a balance between the two and a rod whose action suits you to perfection.

⩗ AT ONE WITH THE WORLD
True bliss. Here I'm wading a Siberian river that's twinkling merrily in the late afternoon sunshine. Grayling are my prey, and I'm looking for them in the little deep pots of water behind each boulder. Accurate casting is important here, and distance, too, as the river is too deep and strong to allow wading far from the margins.

Winning the Battle

You've done all your homework, the fish has taken your fly, and it's a good one. In fact, it's so big and so powerful that your heart is in your mouth, the blood is pounding through your temples, your knees are beginning to shake, and your mouth is going dry. How do you ensure that you're triumphant and that your hopes don't melt like snowflakes in the sea?

• First, try to avoid being seen by the fish. Very many big fish of all species will not immediately realize there is danger on first being hooked. Once they see the angler, or the angler's boat, then the fireworks really begin.

• It's particularly important to remain as inconspicuous as possible when it comes to the final landing stage of the battle. It's surprising how many fish can summon up energy for a last charge. A tired hook hold or a frayed line might just give at this last moment.

• Always keep calm and don't panic. If you lose your head you will lose your fish.

• If a big fish is close to danger, say rapids or a weir pool, try "walking" the fish. To do this, you simply hold the rod at right angles to the river and walk smoothly, slowly, and steadily upriver. The chances are that the fish, puzzled, will follow

and you will be able to lead it out of danger.

• With a running fish, if it's a big one, you simply have to let it go—though hopefully not over the tail of a pool into rough water where there's always a chance of the line getting caught around rocks.

• Make a fish work for every yard of line that it takes from you by putting on the maximum pressure that your tackle will stand. Exert this pressure by tightening down the drag of your reel or simply slowing the revolving drum with the palm of your hand. In extreme cases, a glove will avoid burning.

• It's vital to know when and how to put the pressure on a fish. During a run you will begin to sense that the fish is slowing down and tiring. At this point begin to increase the pressure noticeably. Hopefully the fish will come to a dead stop. It might rise in the water and even splash on the surface—a dangerous moment, and one to be avoided by keeping the rod low, perhaps even parallel to the water.

• You must know pretty accurately what your tackle will withstand in terms of pressure, and you mustn't be afraid to go to the limits. It's usual to see timid anglers playing

◄ THE CRITICAL MOMENT
Usually this moment would not be too critical because all Simon would need to do is bend down, grip the barbless hook with his forceps and allow the fish, in this case an Arctic char, to swim away free. Indeed, if the fish came off at this moment it would be no great problem to him. But not in this case. We're camping in Greenland and we're hungry. Our supplies have run out and this fish represents one of our last chances for a half-decent supper, so Simon has to gently draw the fish toward him, keeping the line tight the whole time.

fish with rods only half bent. The length of the battle will be increased enormously to the detriment of the fish's health. A weak hook hold is also much more likely to give. Be confident in your tackle and really go for it in the fight. Never let a fish dominate you.

• A serious problem is a big fish that settles out in mid-stream where the water is quick and deep. It can settle and clamp itself so firmly that you might think that the fish has gone and you are hooked to the bottom. This is very probably not the case, and once you feel the dullest kick you will know that you are still hooked in. Now you must begin to pump. Take hold of the rod, up from the butt around the first eye. Pull gently but firmly upward. As soon as your rod is vertical, or even a little over your shoulder, wind in quickly as you lower the tip toward the water. Repeat this process as often as you can and you will find that the fish gently moves toward you, hardly aware of what's going on. Pumping is one of the most vital arts in landing a big fish, so learn it and practice it with confidence.

• Always be aware. Keep your eyes wide open during the fight and don't develop tunnel vision. Keep looking around, looking for potential snags that could prove dangerous in the later stages of the fight. Be aware of patches of slack water where you might position a boat or try to lead a fish. Be aware of any possible sandy, shelving landing areas that you can make for when the fight looks to be coming to an end.

• Let's suppose a fish is hooked and you've got line hanging loose around your feet. Let the flowing line run

through your fingers, but remember to exert pressure on the fish as it does so. Always make sure that line hanging loose during the retrieve doesn't snag around bankside vegetation or your own clothing. If this happens, a quick-running fish will pull the line tight and you won't be able to give it any extra.

• Keeping your line free is particularly important on a boat, when fishing for bonefish for example. Keep your decks clear of clutter so there's nothing to foul the line.

• If a fish becomes seemingly irretrievably weeded, hand lining can often work. Reel in until everything is tight and point the rod as directly as possible to where the fish is snagged. Now get hold of the line between the reel and the first rod ring and pull it backward and forward in a sawing motion.

You will find this exerts far more pressure on the snagged fish than the rod itself can muster. What you'll often find is that the fish in a big blanket of weeds begins to come toward you slowly.

• If a river fish is snagged in weeds, don't try to pull it upstream. Instead, get downstream of the fish and pull in the direction of the current.

• When you are landing a fish, never net it and remove it from the water if it's going to be released. Instead, draw it into the shallowest of margins and kneel down beside it. Slip the hook free with forceps and guide it back to deeper water once it has recovered its strength. If a fish is to be killed, then do the job neatly and cleanly and precisely with the right tool and don't rummage around for a rock!

• Finally, always make sure that you are using the right strength tackle for the job. There's no point putting hooks into fish that you know you're never going to be able to land. Also, if you have any doubts about your leaders, your hooks, or your knots, then replace or retie immediately. It's essential that you have absolute confidence in your tackle.

◀ FEELING FOR THE FLATS
Magnus is pictured here about to slip the hook on one of his first bonefish. There are few branches of fly fishing that demand such quick, positive, accurate casting. You wade the Flats with your guide and then he spots a group of bonefish, probably traveling fast. You see them, too, and you have to put the fly in exactly the right position in front of them. Chances are there's a breeze, and it's highly probable you'll only get the one chance. Screw up, and your guide will give you the most critical of looks.

PRACTICE

THE PREPARATION HAS BEEN DONE. YOU'VE NOW GOT THE RIGHT TACKLE AND SOME CONFIDENCE IN THE WATER YOU'RE GOING TO FISH. REMEMBER THAT CONDITIONS CAN CHANGE FROM MINUTE TO MINUTE— AWARENESS AND ADAPTABILITY ARE THE KEYS TO SUCCESSFUL FISHING.

FLY FISHING IN STILL WATER

ALL STILL WATER OFFERS DIFFERENT CHALLENGES. THE FISH MIGHT BE OBVIOUS IN A SMALL POOL, BUT THEY CAN BE DIFFICULT TO TEMPT IF THERE'S A LOT OF FISHING PRESSURE. ALTERNATIVELY, ON HUGE LAKES LOCATION IS THE KEY AND YOU NEED TO HAVE A REAL AWARENESS OF WHERE THE FISH ARE. THIS VARIETY IS WHAT KEEPS FLY FISHERS GOING BACK TO STILL WATER SEASON AFTER SEASON.

On a small still water, the best time of the year is almost certainly late spring through to early summer and then early autumn. Ideally, you're looking for a mild, overcast day with a light breeze. If you can, avoid weekends and holidays because on small fisheries the fishing pressure can have decidedly negative consequences. In fact, when phoning to book a ticket, it's not a bad idea to ask just how many people are likely to be out on any particular day.

Don't be in a rush to speed to the nearest fishable point. Take your time. Walk around the water. Above all, watch for fish and look for areas that are less pressured. Perhaps these areas are difficult to cast into because of trees or reeds, but you can bet that's where older, wilier fish will have taken up residence.

Small waters can be intense and the fish can be suspicious, so don't do anything to alarm them further. Some might snicker at your ultra-cautious approach, but let them. Who

➤ PARADISE FOUND
Lakes come in all shapes and sizes. This is quite a new water, but the fish, with species like bass, are coming on quickly. It's going to be a magnificent water to fish, full of contours and features. There are also many drowned trees, which all species adore either for shelter or for ambush purposes.

➤ MAKING A START
The water is all but empty, and that gives me the freedom to roam. Above all else, if there hasn't been anybody else on the water all day, the fish everywhere will be more relaxed, less likely to spook, probably coming close inshore to feed.

cares, providing you have the last laugh? So, put your tackle together well away from the waterside and if you get any tangles, or even when you change your fly, slowly creep out of sight to deal with the problem.

Always start with good, proven, standard patterns such as short casts covering the water in a radial, clock-face pattern. Don't be in too much of a hurry. Let the fly sink well down before starting a retrieve, and always keep that retrieve as perky and lifelike as you possibly can. If your concentration sags, your chances, too, will droop.

Keep your rod slightly off to one side, with the tip close to the water and the line straight to the fly. This

➢ FEELING FOR A TAKE

I would generally have my left hand much closer to the rod than this so that I could feel for a bite more intimately and be quicker on a strike. However, I've kicked off using a dry fly. There are fish in the surface layers picking off moths and crane flies, and when a trout comes up for a big fly like this it's best not to be in too much of a hurry. The ploy, however, doesn't work and I'm soon back to nymphs.

way, you'll move the fly in a more lifelike fashion, and you'll hook more fish on the take as well. In all still-water fishing, a major reason for failure is not detecting the takes in the first place.

The depth that you're fishing and the speed of your retrieve are always much more important than the pattern of fly you're using.

➢ AND IT WORKS

The change to a large nymph works almost immediately. Although there are fish showing at the surface, they are reluctant to feed, and by getting down deep I experience a couple of quick tugs followed by a long, slow, unmissable pull. I don't, however, think that I've fished particularly well. It's been an easy morning, and I haven't really been pushed into extreme techniques.

Have confidence in your fly; then forget it and concentrate on exactly how you're working it.

Keep your eyes wide open, and if you see a rise or a cruising fish, immediately cast to it. Don't land the fly right on top of the fish, but just in front of it so that it will come across the sinking fly as naturally as possible.

Enjoy your day. OK, you've bought your ticket, but don't bust a

◄ COMING TO HAND

I don't need a net for this one. It's going straight back, wiser from its experience, so all I need to do is kneel down and draw it into the margins in front of me. No sweat, no bother.

gut to get a limit—if a catch limit is still in force on the water. The more you relax and let the character of the water seep into you, the more you'll form a connection, the more you'll understand, and the more successful you'll become.

➤ INVALUABLE ACCESSORY

With a barbless or semi-barbed hook it's the easiest of matters to flick it clear using a hemostat. The fish is bemused all right, and tired, but there's no blood and no lasting damage. The fish will learn from its mistake and will be more difficult to catch in the future, and what we're all after in our fishing is a challenge.

STAY OR MOVE?

Let's say that you have a water pretty much to yourself. Well, should you fish specific areas intently or should you keep on the move?

- A lot depends on what the fish are doing. If you see plenty of fish rising in front of you then it's worth staying to work out a strategy.
- If the water appears absolutely dead, then, if it's rainbows you're after, it's probably wise to keep on the move, looking for a group of fish willing to make a mistake.
- Browns, however, are a slightly different kettle of fish, pardon the pun. With them, on smaller commercial waters, it's often better to settle down in an area that you know is likely to produce fish and concentrate on it intently. Work an imitative pattern very carefully, very close to the bottom, in slow, short retrieves. In fact, the whole cast can often take 10 or even 15 minutes to fish out. Look for the slightest possible signs of a take. Often the line just lifts a fraction but it's enough to put a hook into a big fish.
- Learn from your mistakes.

➤ A SPLIT-SECOND POSE

I'm lifting the fish out of the water for a moment so that the photographer can snap away. But it is only for a moment, in order to do the fish as little harm as possible. Perhaps we shouldn't sentimentalize about stocked fish, as many end up on the plate, but it's a good idea to take this care and consideration for our catch with us wherever we go.

The Year on Large Waters

Whether you're on a lake, a lough, a loch, or a reservoir, there are certain guiding principles that hold true and can be taken from one to the other.

The early season can be cold and dour, but you'll want to get out and make a start. Preferably you're looking for an overcast, comparatively mild day when fish are more likely to be moving and you're less likely to freeze your hands off. It's important to keep mobile during the early season because the fish could be anywhere. They won't yet have settled into predictable patrol patterns, and you'll come across groups of fish all over the place. In general, aim for water around 10 feet deep that is reachable from the bank.

In all probability, you will be using heavier, sinking lines, possibly with larger flies. Remember to roll cast a sinking line out of the water before trying to lift it to the overhead cast. Otherwise, a

▲ A WEALTH OF SPECIES

Lough Melvin is one of Europe's most spectacular waters, with many species of fish to be caught. Salmon enter the lough, and you'll also find ferox trout, brown trout, and sonaghan trout, which are small—up to 1½ pounds or so—but streamlined and silvery and looking almost like sea trout. There are also the famous gillaroos—hugely spotted, growing to 3 or 4 pounds, and feeding mainly on snails.

▼ THE RESERVOIR SCENE

Fly fishing on large, artificial waters has totally changed the nature of the sport. For example, because of the depths that are involved, new, fast-sink lines and tactics have been evolved. The modern breed of angler fishing these large waters never gives up. Fish will be pursued from the surface to depths of 60 feet or more according to the season and the weather conditions on any particular day.

tangle and a potentially dangerous situation could result. Remember to cast slowly, too, because it takes time for heavy lines and flies to get up to speed. If you are using a sinking line at this time of the year, be sure you know its sink rate so that you're sure at what level you are fishing. When the line lands, count it down in seconds in order to search out different depths. Make a mental note of how far down you are when you connect with the fish, for future reference. If you're fishing a lure, retrieve with long, steady pulls and

keep retrieving until an ideal casting length of line comes back to the rod. Have confidence in your fly. When you're certain that you've explored a range of depths without success it's better to change the color rather than the pattern.

What will the fish actually be feeding on in the early part of the season? The answer can be varied. In Lough Corrib in Ireland, for example, early season floods often scour out the feeder streams and wash minnows into the lough. The trout enjoy feeding on them, and

minnow patterns work well at this time. Otherwise, trout are probably down deep, feeding among the stones and dead weeds looking for beetles, shrimp, and any nymphs. That's where you've got to use imitations.

⩔ MAYFLY MADNESS
It doesn't matter what still water you are fishing, the two weeks or so of the mayfly hatch probably represent the very cream of the sport, the highlight of your year. It's when these big, succulent flies hatch that the very largest of trout are likely to come up and take an imitation. The obvious lesson here is never to fish with too light a leader.

In early spring things are likely to change as the first hatches, most notably of midges, take place. The trout will now be settling into steadier feeding patterns and fishing can become somewhat more delicate. The fish are gaining condition during this period, often gorging on the vast numbers of midges hatching. Look for them over deeper areas, probably where there are weeds or silt on the bottom.

As we move into late spring–early summer we're still not done with the midges, but olives begin to appear in numbers and the fish will often switch to them. While you can take numbers of fish from the surface on dry olive patterns, it is inadvisable to neglect the sinking line for a great percentage of any successful day.

The olives stagger on, but some time toward the very end of spring, depending on the weather and geography, the mayflies begin to appear. In Ireland, for example, this is the start of festival fishing. These gloriously beautiful and highly succulent flies take over, and fishing on the dap, especially, is the vital form of presentation. Everything eats the mayfly—salmon if they're in the water, and even pike! If there's ever a glut period, this is it.

⅄ THE LAKE BED

If you're really going to fish any still water, however large, to its absolute limits, it's important to know what the lake bed is composed of. Large rocks, for example, can often be the hiding place for some very big trout indeed. Gravel and small stones are frequently favored by salmon if they can gain access. Larger stones are very likely to attract snails and, therefore, bottom-feeding fish. Muddy holes are frequently homes of the bloodworm. Of course, in very deep waters it is difficult to be absolutely sure what's happening 100 or even 40 feet beneath your boat. That's why, on the really big lakes, a guide is such a valuable companion.

STILL-WATER MIDGE TACTICS

There's no more exciting way of taking fish in stillwaters than off the surface or immediately beneath it, and this is where midge fishing is such a central technique. You can expect to pick up trout, especially, all the way through the season, and even in winter if you're prepared to go deep.

1 Late in the day sees the most vigorous action to midges. Look for areas where the day's breeze has blown a covering of scum until there's a thick surface film. The midges will have trouble hatching here and the trout know it. Look for swirls, heads, backs, dorsals, and tails, and listen for that distinctive smacking sound.

2 Start with either one or two midges on your leader. Begin with a hook size of 10 to 14. Black and red are traditional. The new epoxy-tied midges are particularly deadly, with their flash and natural look. If you don't get any action, then make the effort to change color, size, and materials.

3 Begin with a leader strength of 3 or 4 pounds breaking strain, but if you're fishing a water with big fish then scale up, and if you decide to fish on at night, when the biggest fish of all are likely to feed, then 7 or even 8 pounds isn't too much.

4 You can grease the leader to within a few inches of the top fly. This is important to prevent the midges from sinking too deep, and you can also watch the floating leader for any signs of a take. Alternatively, use a large dry fly, both as a sight indicator and as a controller, so the flies don't sink too deep. A Muddler is a good one, or even a crane fly.

5 Take your time and try to identify the route individual fish are taking. Once you do this, you can place a midge a yard or so in front of it and twitch it back across its nose while it's on its natural patrol route.

6 Keep everything as tight as you can. Watch your leader or top fly like a hawk.

You'll need to do this in failing light conditions especially. If you can, cast westward, toward the setting sun. You'll find this gives you just a little bit more light on the water.

7 Either leave the midges stationary in the surface film or give them slight twitches. If feeding activity is really frenzied, a slow, continual retrieve can produce smash takes.

8 Don't be in too much of a hurry to leave at the end of the evening. If the rules allow it, continue fishing into darkness. This has proved particularly effective on some of the big western loughs in Ireland, where some of the guys stay out until 2 o'clock in the morning.

After the mayfly, there's often a lull in fishing through mid-summer. In Ireland, many of the fishermen will move off to fish for salmon and sea trout but, since the introduction of English reservoir techniques, more and more are staying on to enjoy superb sport. Late summer can see some tremendous sedge hatches. It's also in August that many fish are down deep, feeding energetically on the banks of scuds. Locating the fish now can be difficult, and in many conditions you'll need a sinking line.

Perhaps the best scud sport anywhere is provided by the sonaghan trout of Lough Melvin, which straddles the border between Northern Ireland and the Republic of Ireland. Sonaghan are rather like sea trout, averaging 12 ounces to a pound, and they fight frenetically. They are obsessive scud feeders. If the weather is bright the scuds will be down and they will stay there, too, during heavy rain. You'll need intermediate lines with sink tips. Choose black flies with a bit of flash on the tail. The Bibio is good and the Clan Chief is a real Irish favorite. Don't cast long, because the sonaghan hit fast and you can miss at least 40 takes before you land a single fish unless you're really tight and in touch.

These sonaghan highlight one of the biggest problems in the fly-fisher's world—detecting and striking takes. At least with the sonaghan you generally know when one has nipped at the fly, even if converting a take into a securely hooked fish is a different matter altogether. The major problem on so many waters is simply detecting the take in the first place. This can be especially difficult on stillwaters when there is little or no current and it's harder to keep a direct line to the fly. Believe me, it's quite possible to have a take and know nothing about it at all, so concentrate with all your senses and really focus on the line.

> ➤ CRYSTAL CLEAR

A big, crystal-clear lake on a baking hot day will produce some of the most difficult conditions that you will ever come across. Leo is standing close to the shore, but you'll notice from the angle of his line that he's casting not far out into the lake but a long way down the margins. This is because fish will often come into marginal weeds even when the weather is hot and even where the water is shallow. They are looking for the food that the margins attract, and if they're not frightened by a footstep or a falling line they can be surprisingly easy to tempt. The other, more obvious approach is to search for fish way out in much deeper water, probably with a sinking line.

> ➤ THE MOMENT OF TRUTH

The guile of a fish depends on whether it is wild or stocked, educated or naïve, pressured or unpressured, and upon the clarity of the water itself. Certainly, the number of fish that follow a fly and then veer away is far greater than the number that end up taking the fly.

THE ART OF DAPPING

Dapping is traditionally associated with the big Irish loughs in the spring when the mayflies are up. Boats drift with the wind across comparatively shallow, rocky ground where the mayflies proliferate. Long rods are used, along with silk lines that catch the breeze. At the end of the leader, live mayflies are commonly attached to a hook or, failing that, imitative patterns are used.

Rods are traditionally 14 to 16 feet long, and telescopic models are favored so that they can be extended or shortened according to conditions. However, a long trout or light salmon rod can be used.

Lines are generally made of dapping floss because they catch the wind better. Attach this to 100 yards or so of nylon backing in readiness for a really big fish taking off. The length of the dapping floss varies according to the state of the wind and length of rod, but 6 feet is generally

considered about right. Use a short leader and don't go too fine if big fish are expected. You can catch the mayflies yourself or, in Ireland, buy them from local boys. Thread anything between one and six mayflies on a hook sized 8 to 12.

This is really a boat-fishing method, although it can occasionally be done from the bank. Let the boat drift, sometimes miles on larger waters, hold the rod vertically, pay out the dapping line until it clears the tip ring, and then lower the rod so that the mayflies are skipping on the surface of the wave. Don't drag them about unnaturally. The aim is to make them appear as lively and unsuspicious as possible, and the same applies with the artificial. Try twitching the rod tip from time to time so that the fly skits from one side to the other.

When you get a take, don't be in too much of a hurry to strike. Sometimes

the trout will submerge the flies before sipping them in. (Sometimes they will merely splash at the mayflies—real or imitation—in an attempt to drown them before taking them, in which case do nothing, because they will probably return.) Delay your strike until the line goes out and tightens, and then merely lift into the hooked fish.

This isn't simply a method for the mayfly season. You can dap with any large naturals, such as grasshoppers, sedges, and crane flies. Equally, try the method with the imitations of these. Don't go thinking that this is a method restricted to Ireland alone. It's of use on all large stillwaters where regulations allow.

A decent breeze is generally considered important for dapping, as you do need a bit of a wave, and you can even dap in really strong wind conditions, but don't go out if you sense danger.

◁ CHANGING LEVELS

Large waters, and reservoirs especially, are very prone to changes in water level. On many of these stillwaters a rise or fall of 20 feet or so in just a few days is not unusual. This really has the effect of pushing the fish about. For example, if heavy rain falls and the lake rises rapidly, expect to find fish flocking into the margins, where all manner of terrestrial insects will be trapped. Notice I said "terrestrial": Fish can become quite preoccupied at times like this and refuse the more normal imitative offerings we are used to fishing. When a lake is low, it's also a good idea to make a note of any obvious features, so that you can fish to them when the level rises again.

From late summer and into autumn, you'll find that many of the trout are beginning to feed on fry, and fish patterns worked quite quickly really come into their own. Watch for small fish jumping from the water as trout attack them.

This is also the time of the year when crane flies proliferate and many big fish come to take them from the surface. Fishing the crane flies is hugely exciting—one minute your fly is just hanging there and the next second there's a great explosion and you're playing a fish that's seemingly come out of nowhere.

In Ireland, a lot of crane-fly fishing is done on the dap with live insects, but large artificials work very well. Learn to twitch them from time to time to impart life, and don't worry too much if they begin to sink into the surface film looking like a crippled, dying insect. You can leave the fly static on the water, simply keeping in touch with it as your boat, if you're afloat, approaches the fly. Alternatively, you can twitch it slowly back toward you in a faltering retrieve. Keep an open mind and try both tactics.

High-Altitude Waters

Wherever in the world there is high-altitude, barren moorland you are likely to come across splashes of water anything between half an acre and 30 or more acres in extent that hold trout. Frequently, partly because of the altitude and partly because of the poorness of the soil, the trout are small, but this isn't always the case and there are some amazing discoveries to be made.

Of course, making the best use of these gems calls for a certain amount of independence. These are waters that are frequently totally unfished or barely fished. They are usually miles from the nearest road and often they can only be reached over hostile terrain. You have no way of knowing what the water holds, and there's little or no local

➢ GOING AFLOAT
On large waters, don't place all your trust in your engine and always make sure that you have oars and oarlocks with you. Also, never go out without a life preserver. Look, too, at the angler opposite—he'd be far safer sitting down. Avoid standing up in a boat, as you're more likely to pitch over the side. Boat safety is to be taken seriously.

⋎ IT'S A HARD LIFE
Bright sun, clear water, and next to no ripple—one of the most difficult fly-fishing situations. A peaked cap and polarizing glasses help kill the glare, so at least you can see any twitch on your fly line and, possibly, fish moving in the water itself. At times like this you've got to keep experimenting until you find fish. Try different sink-rate lines. Keep your eyes open for any surface activity. Make sure all your actions are gentle and controlled. Try to rock the boat as little as possible.

➢ INTENSITY

It is important to focus intensely on locating the fish, present them with what they want, and then concentrate hawk-like on detecting takes. You'll see here that Basil is totally alive to what's going on—his eyes are glued to his fly line and to the point where the leader meets the water. His sense of touch is also acute, and he's in the perfect position to react to even the most gentle of takes.

knowledge. The weather can be unpredictable. These are barren, desolate places that demand a brave approach.

Safety is a major consideration. Don't go out if there's any doubt about bad weather coming in, and be particularly wary of fog and mist. Have a really detailed map with you, plus a compass that you're able to use. Take warm clothing, even in the height of summer—the weather can change dramatically very quickly. Take plenty of water, especially if you're walking distances with kit in hot weather. Don't carry more than you need and don't encumber yourself with unwanted fish as you leave—put them back and make the walk home easier. Always tell somebody at base camp where you're going and when you expect to be back. Don't fish for longer than you've told them—you could endanger people in an unnecessary rescue attempt.

So much for the cautions. What do you actually do when you get to that water that was, just a couple of hours ago, a splash of blue somewhere above the 3,000-foot contour line on the map? Well, obviously, keep your eyes open for any sign of moving or feeding fish, and watch out for fish-eating birds giving you a clue to location. Look for any weed beds, lily pads (yes, even at that altitude!), sand bars, in-flowing streams, and obvious drop-offs—anything that gives you a clue as to where to begin.

You will probably not see many fish rise, because the waters are likely to be comparatively poor. Try, to start with, fishing as deep as you can with anything small and black. Move it slowly, trying to represent any one of a score of insect forms that the trout might recognize. Work the shoreline diligently. Cover all the water in front of you in a rhythmic,

⋏ CHANGES FOR THE BETTER

Basil still has a dry net, but conditions are improving. The sun is sinking and the wind has risen a little giving a perfect chop to the water. Basil has seen a couple of fish moving in or around the surface film and now he's dancing flies—a team of midges—in the critical area. His concentration is intense, but this time his rod is held higher so he has less fly line resting on the lake's surface. He is direct to the two midges and can react at once to any interest.

BOAT-ANGLING TIPS

- If you are on a large, unknown water with possibly dangerous rocks, go out with a local boatman, at least for the first few occasions.
- Some larger lakes are like small seas, and bad weather can spell real danger, so avoid it. Don't go out in a boat unless you are confident, and always wear a life preserver, even if you can swim (and I strongly recommend that you should be able to).
- Even if your engine is the most reliable in the world, ensure you have oars. On very large waters, a map and a compass can be useful.
- If you're on your own, an electric outboard is very helpful, especially if you're fishing midges. It's hard to row and cast to feeding fish at the same time.
- Think carefully about your drifts. Consider the direction and speed of the wind and the ground you want to fish over.
- Generally, you can dap or fish most wet and dry flies on an unrestricted drift. If you want to fish nymphs or midges you might well want to slow your boat down using a sea anchor. When you are fishing normal wet flies on the drift you have

to retrieve just fast enough to keep in touch with them, but not so fast that you're pulling them at an unnatural speed through the water.
- Don't forget to lift your rod tip and let the flies dibble close to the surface before removing them to re-cast. Trout will very often follow right to the boat itself.
- Boat etiquette is important. If you get a feeling that you're harming the sport of others in any way, stop immediately. For example, don't drop anchor if you're on a drift with others behind you. Never motor through a drift that either you or others are working. Instead, go back upwind in a wide arc before settling back to fish in line. Never go close to a bank angler, especially with your engine on. If you're approaching a quiet bay at sunset where others are fishing, cut your engine speed right down to avoid noise and wake. If your boat is hired, leave it as tidy as when you picked it up (or tidier, come to that). Remove all trash, even if it doesn't belong to you.
- Always switch off your engine and lift it up before gliding in to a rocky, shallow landing place, and always leave your boat in a safe position. Make sure it is properly

tied up to something immovable on the bank. Don't leave a boat washing around if there's a swell or if a rising wind is forecast. Try to pull the boat as far as possible out of the water where you know it will be safe.
- Sitting on hard wooden seats all day long can be uncomfortable. Think about taking a cushion, or even your own fishing chair if the boat is big enough.
- It's never a bad idea to have your own set of oarlocks in the car in case they're missing on your hire-boat.
- Keep a spare set of dry clothes in your car. You never know when you might get a soaking and it may be a long journey home.
- Be sure to take plenty of food and warm drink with you... it can be cold out in a brisk wind.
- If it's hot, make sure you're well covered up and rub sunscreen onto any exposed parts. Sunburn can be a much greater problem on water than land.
- Remember that voices carry very clearly over water. I'm sure you'd never say anything rude, but keep your voice down anyway for the good of all, including the fishing.

methodical way, and then move 30 yards or so along the bank. Keep going until you find fish. Don't be panicked into changing flies all the time—it's more important to work them intelligently than it is to worry about what's on the end. After all, these probably aren't educated fish and they aren't likely to be too wary of your tackle. However, they will be wary of you. Humans will not be part of their daily life, so move and cast with care. If you're wading, don't splash about.

Still no joy? Try a fish-pattern fly worked back quickly in midwater or

nearer the surface. Failing that, try a large terrestrial pattern fished dry—a crane fly is the obvious one to go for here. Let it drift on the wave and twitch it back to you in a very slow retrieve.

Keep going. Fish in waters like this are notoriously unpredictable and can suddenly come on the feed out of nowhere. If you're not endangering yourself or others, try to stay on until the last of the light. This is often the prime period on these waters.

Don't risk going too light. I can't begin to tell you what to expect, but

you could be in for a surprise. Many of the fish might only be a hand's span, but it's quite possible you will hit into something that takes your breath away. People do, all over the place, more often than you think.

Now this may sound dreadfully selfish, but if you do hit lucky with some unexpected fish, then keep quiet about it. Tell very close friends, perhaps, but don't broadcast the news far and wide, because stocks of wild fish can frequently be much less dense than you'd think and they can be quickly and disastrously thinned out.

SPAWNING STREAMS
Not all inflowing streams attract spawning fish, but local knowledge will direct you to those that do. You'll often find fish massing near the mouth of spawning streams toward the end of the season. They're very catchable then.

CONTOURS
Try and build up an impression of important contours on the lake's bottom. You'll often find fish feeding along the ledge where the shallows drop off to the deeps.

ROCKS
Look out for rocks, weeds, fallen trees, sunken boats—anything that breaks up the contour of the lake bed. Find a feature, and you're sure to find a fish—especially if it's bass that you're after.

A Big Lake

You can fly fish in waters the size of the Caspian Sea, but most lakes and reservoirs aren't quite that big! By big stillwaters I'm thinking primarily of places probably a mile or more in length, and though they may look daunting to beginners, they still have their features.

Always bear safety firmly in mind. Most large waters are best fished from boats, which can be dangerous if the weather is unkind or there's a flaw in your boating technique or equipment. Be particularly careful of waters that possess a great number of rocks just under the surface of the water— these can be very difficult to spot, especially in poor conditions.

The weather is crucial on these large waters and a big wind can make certain areas unfishable. A breeze of between 2 and 4 mph in strength is ideal; this makes drifting long lanes of water possible. It always helps if you have a boatman to keep you on course, but two anglers ought to be able to operate quite successfully if they use teamwork. The great advantage of drifting is that large areas of the water are opened up and explored with the minimum of physical effort.

Cast with the wind behind you to the front and side of the boat. You will have to retrieve, of course, faster than the boat is moving. Drifting

works very well with the dapping method. On large waters some drifts can take virtually a whole morning and you can often cover several miles of water and hundreds of feeding fish.

Local knowledge can be important for all manner of reasons. Most vitally, the locals will know which areas of the lake are particularly prolific at particular moments in time.

However, there are still age-old rules that the visiting angler or beginner can follow and these should catch him or her some fish. For example, if it's a hot, bright day then from mid-morning to the late

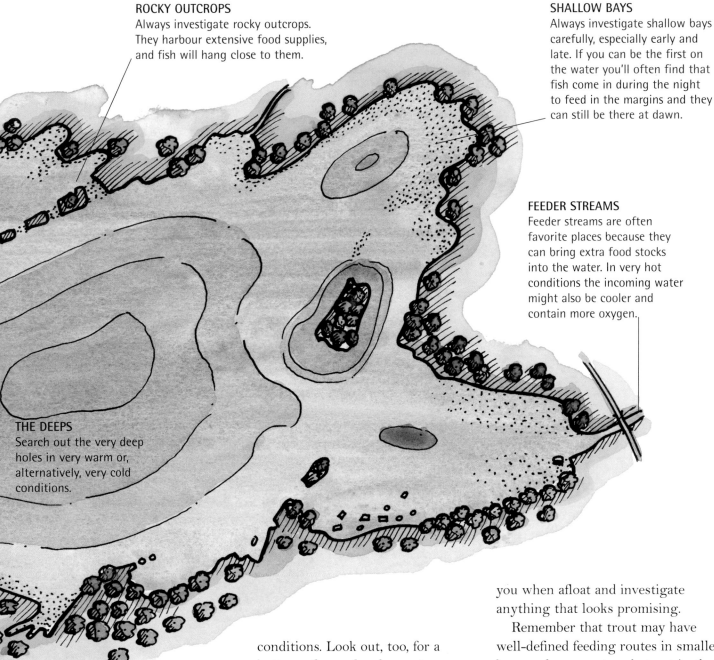

ROCKY OUTCROPS
Always investigate rocky outcrops. They harbour extensive food supplies, and fish will hang close to them.

SHALLOW BAYS
Always investigate shallow bays carefully, especially early and late. If you can be the first on the water you'll often find that fish come in during the night to feed in the margins and they can still be there at dawn.

FEEDER STREAMS
Feeder streams are often favorite places because they can bring extra food stocks into the water. In very hot conditions the incoming water might also be cooler and contain more oxygen.

THE DEEPS
Search out the very deep holes in very warm or, alternatively, very cold conditions.

afternoon many fish are likely to be found in the deepest part of the water where there is an element of cool and protection from the sun. Fast-sinking lines can get down to the fish and produce results under the most unpromising conditions. Alternatively, look for shallow, sheltered bays where there's a good amount of cover and plenty of natural food. If there is aquatic vegetation, you'll often find trout close in, feeding hard, even in bright

conditions. Look out, too, for a bottom of gravel or large stones. These are particularly useful in the spring before major fly hatches because they harbour colonies of water shrimp and snails.

You'll often find that bays fish well very early in the morning or late at night. This is especially so if they haven't been pressured during the course of the day and the fish haven't been driven from the shallow water. Above all, keep your eyes open. Look for rises and even the activity of waterfowl—it's a good idea to take a pair of binoculars with

you when afloat and investigate anything that looks promising.

Remember that trout may have well-defined feeding routes in smaller bays on larger waters, but out in the main body of the lake it's highly likely that the fish will be very mobile, constantly on the fin looking for food. It's the same with salmon running through a lake—chances are they'll have well-defined traveling zones and places where they like to rest up. Inevitably, local knowledge plays a huge part in pinpointing these places. If you're new to a big water it really does make sense to go out with a guide for at least the first day or two. He'll fill you with ideas and, above all, confidence.

Small Still Waters

Some of the very best still waters in the world are slightly enlarged puddles, but their lack of size doesn't mean that they can't be rich in food life, and they often produce huge fish.

Many of these small waters are commercially run and stocked, but not all. In wilderness areas, you'll often come across small, wild fisheries. Above all, treat small waters with great respect and think tremendously carefully about your approach. Be careful of marshy banks, for example—a heavy footfall will send out tremors that the fish will feel easily. Make use of trees and bushes around the banks and use them as ambush points.

On small waters, it's frequently possible to stalk individual fish, and if you see one that interests you, spend as much time as it takes to build up a picture of its patrol route. You can then place a fly in front of it before it actually arrives.

Observe small water etiquette. Don't, for example, remain on your favorite point all day. Others might wish to fish there. Don't move in too close to an angler already fishing—he might be stalking a fish that's very special to him. Keep your voice down because that could spook somebody else's fish.

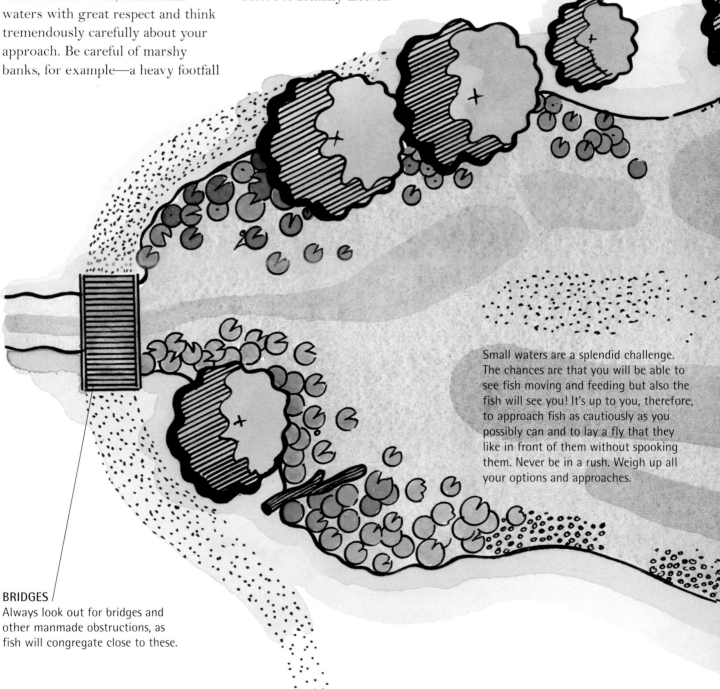

Small waters are a splendid challenge. The chances are that you will be able to see fish moving and feeding but also the fish will see you! It's up to you, therefore, to approach fish as cautiously as you possibly can and to lay a fly that they like in front of them without spooking them. Never be in a rush. Weigh up all your options and approaches.

BRIDGES
Always look out for bridges and other manmade obstructions, as fish will congregate close to these.

TREES
You will often find fish cruising and feeding under overhanging trees. Look for terrestrial insects falling from the branches and try to imitate them.

THE SHALLOWS
The shallows are particularly frequented early and late in the day when the water is at its quietest. The shallows are especially attractive if they're of sand or gravel.

LILIES
You'll often find fish feeding among lily pads. They scrape the snails and tiny insects from the underneath of the pads and from the stems.

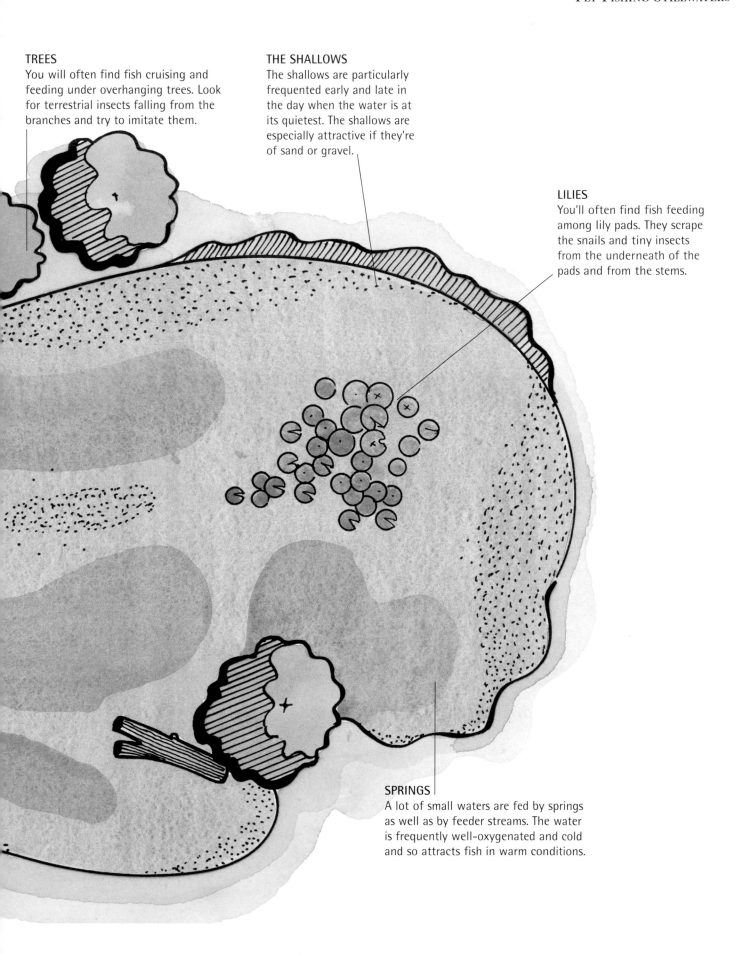

SPRINGS
A lot of small waters are fed by springs as well as by feeder streams. The water is frequently well-oxygenated and cold and so attracts fish in warm conditions.

FLY FISHING RIVERS

THERE'S A WHOLE RANGE OF JOYS TO RIVER FISHING, NOT LEAST THE BUBBLING, SINGING ENVIRONMENT ITSELF. SOME ANGLERS LIKE TO GET CLOSE-UP AND INTIMATE ON SMALL, CRYSTAL RIVERS, WHILE OTHERS PREFER LONG CASTING AND BIG TAKES AT DISTANCE. WHETHER YOU'RE INTO THE MAJESTIC RIVER OR THE GURGLING STREAM, THE APPROACH AND THE SKILLS ARE BASICALLY THE SAME.

Above all, in the vast majority of cases, you are pursuing wild fish, and that's one of the real joys of it all. However, wild fish nearly always mean fish stocks under pressure, so return almost everything in a caring, humane fashion and create as little stress on the river as you possibly can.

Approaching a Creek

My definition of a creek is something no more than 3 or 4 yards across and frequently less. You'll find them curling through meadows or woodland, often with many sharp bends and a continuing succession of small pools and fast riffles. The water will generally be clear and the fish are almost certainly wild. Primarily you'll be expecting trout.

The first thing to bear in mind is your gear. Travel light—a 7-foot rod should be enough, with perhaps a 3- or 4-weight line. A few nymphs, a selection of dries, your glasses, drab clothing, chest waders, and you're off.

From there on, it's all about true creepy-crawly stuff. Make good use of every bit of bankside cover that you can. Learn to cast on your knees, on your stomach, or even on your back. Watch carefully for rising fish. In the deeper pools, shuffle to the bankside and spend 10 or 15 minutes looking through the water until you see fish. Watch to see how they are lying and upon what they're feeding. Then work out your strategy.

➤ BIG FISH
A magnificent salmon that's obviously brought a great deal of pleasure to its captor. The angler is treating it carefully, holding it just above the waterline.

There are few, if any, rules of etiquette when it comes to creek fishing. You can fish up, down, or across – whatever you think will best serve your purposes. Try jigging a fly directly beneath your rod tip in deep water under some fallen branches. Don't ignore the quick white water… there can be a lot of food here and trout can be attracted in numbers. Try letting your line and fly just float down with the current to an appealing spot that you can't reach with a direct cast. Once it's there, don't let out any more line, but retrieve with short, tiny tugs.

Look out for places that anglers will never have fished before because of the difficulty, such as long, heavily wooded stretches that you can probably get to with chest waders,

◄ LITTLE FISH
Any fish should be judged in the light of the water it comes from, so if you are fishing little more than a meandering brook, catching a tiny but mature and perfectly formed brown trout like this should be enough for you. Unhook small fish very carefully and remember what the pressure of your fingers can do to such a fragile specimen.

and make your way slowly upstream. Don't be afraid of walking all the way to the limits of the fishery, where the footsteps have died away. Wild fish are wary fish, and the less education they've had the better it is for you.

Above all, take your time and don't rush. Look at the water, watch the fish, consider your approach, and set about your task with patience and delicacy. One wrong move and you may well blow the whole plot.

Approaching Larger Rivers

Here I'm talking about waters from 5 yards wide to 100 yards or more! Obviously, in many cases you're not quite as eyeball-to-eyeball with the fish as you would be on a smaller river, but that doesn't mean to say that you can let your commando skills slip. Larger rivers call for wading or

for longer casting, and you are going to need a bigger rod. Eight- and 9-footers will do for the medium-sized river, but for the really monstrous rivers you'll need anything between 12 and 15 feet if you're going to put out casts of 30 yards or more. Of course, it's worth checking first of all whether such long casts are really necessary. Is there no way of getting closer to your target fish? Long casting can be fun in itself, but the heavier gear will land less softly and could scare fish.

Big rivers have a whole array of features, and it's really good to start by walking your entire beat—even if that means several miles. Leave your rod and just walk, taking mental notes or, even better, sketching a plan of the bankside itself. Look out for islands and the slack water they

create. Look for deep, slow eddies close into the bank. Has a fallen tree created a big, deep, slow pool behind it? Are there any feeder streams entering? These are nearly always top places. Small fish gather to take

➤ AN EXHIBITION OF EXCELLENCE
Moving quickly, quietly, and purposefully, Mick fished a mile or so of river in about two hours, picking fish up here, there, and virtually everywhere he fished. The key on small waters is to keep moving, to keep trying new fish, and to read the river with intense accuracy.

➤ ONE OF LIFE'S LESSONS
I'd been fishing this pool for three hours with bait and hadn't had a bite. Franta, a member of the Czech Fly-Fishing Team, moved in and used his country's nymphing technique to great effect, landing bream, trout, and grayling in a matter of minutes. Never before had I realized that fly could be more efficient than bait.

the insects washed to them, while larger predators mill around in the slightly deeper water. Look for pools beneath waterfalls where the water is deep, strong, and well-oxygenated. Hunt out long, steady glides with a gravel or sand bottom. All your target fish will love to hang here.

The big river can be an awesome proposition, but don't be intimidated. Get to know it, work out its character, and soon it will all begin to make sense. It's the ultimate test of your watercraft, so don't shirk it.

The Dry Fly on a River

You've already learned a little about the hatching flies and how to recognize them. Now it's time to put the theory into practice. You've tied on an imitation that's as close as you can get to the naturals that are around, and you're now going to put it out onto the water. Accuracy is absolutely essential, and many fish will fail to take a dry simply because they haven't seen it. Ensure your casting is as neat and tight as possible. If you're right-handed, put

⩗ WORKING IT OUT
Husband-and-wife team John and Sarah Gilman stand in the margins of a river watching a couple of very impressive bass hunting small fry and insects in the marginal reeds. They're quite happy to take their time to work out a strategy and to decide exactly where to put the right fly to take one of these fine predators.

your right foot forward a little bit. Angle your body forward a fraction. Make sure your elbow is tucked in to your body. Feel the whole cast flow through you—nothing jerky, everything harmonious, your rod close to the side of your head. On the forward cast, as the fly is about to alight, look down the rod as if it were the barrel of a gun pointing at your prey.

There's no need to make yourself cast too far—distance shouldn't be an issue. If you approach your rising fish from behind, so that it is facing away from you, it shouldn't actually see your approach. Trout do have a blind spot behind them so, providing your footfall is soft, you can get close. Remember that most dry-fly captures are made at a distance of between 5 and 10 yards.

Size up the situation before making your first move—try to work out how regularly the trout you are after is rising. Is it very 30, 60, or 90 seconds? Try to put your fly to it at just the moment you think the next rise is likely. Look around—are there any dangerous overhanging branches that could snag your back cast? Is there any troublesome weed that could impede the line floating with the current? Remember that your first cast to a rising trout is almost invariably your best chance, so don't rush it. Make sure it is as perfect as you can make it.

Don't aim the fly directly onto the rise—depending on wind, current, and other variables, try to place it

➤ GET IN LINE
The River Moy at Ballina in Ireland can be crazy at times, especially when the tide is right and the salmon are running up through the town in flotillas. This is when, quite suddenly, the bars empty and everyone heads for the river, either to fish or to watch. It's not fishing in the pastoral sense, but it's exciting and it's productive.

◄ OUT OF SIGHT
You can't even see the river here so you've got to take my word for it that there is one. On a small stream not only must you not be seen but even your rod over the water can cause complete panic and a speedy disappearance of fish. Once again, the ability to cast from a kneeling, or even a lying position, is well demonstrated. David didn't actually catch anything on this particular afternoon but he came extraordinarily close and, given the brightness of the day and the clarity of the water, the session could be counted a success.

about a yard or so upstream, so that it settles nicely and gives the trout plenty of time to see it as it drifts down with the current. Don't aim your cast at the water, but a couple

of feet above it, so that everything falls as softly as you can make it.

Try not to false cast more than you must—the flash of the line will only alarm the fish. If you're in any

doubt about how much line you have out, it's better to land short rather than long. If you put the line over the fish it will bolt without fail.

Watch out for "drag"—the way the current pulls the line and the leader and makes the dry fly skate across the water rather than floating down with it. If the fly lands on slow-moving water and the leader and line on quick water, then you've got an immediate problem. It's often good to wiggle the rod the moment the forward cast has stopped to put a

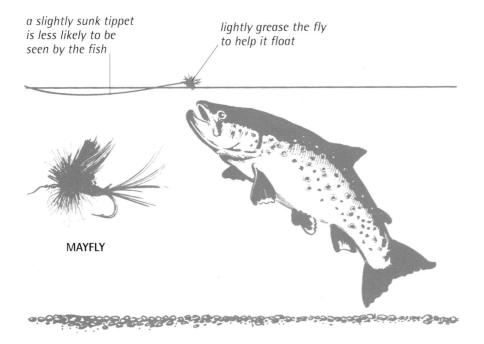

a slightly sunk tippet is less likely to be seen by the fish

lightly grease the fly to help it float

MAYFLY

◄ DRY FLIES
Keep false casts to a minimum, because if you're dry-fly fishing your prey is obviously near the surface and is likely to see the line and the leader flashing backward and forward over its head. Gauge the length of your cast very carefully, because you don't want to lay the fly line over a rising trout. It's better to fall short. Watch the fish that you're targeting very carefully before casting, because you'll find that it has a rhythm, perhaps rising just once every 45 seconds or so. Try to place your dry fly in exactly the right place at exactly the right moment and you're much more likely to have a take. Don't cast directly at the water either, but aim around a couple of feet above it. By doing this you'll find that the fly itself drops a lot more gently upon the water's surface, much more like the real thing. As the fly actually hits the surface, try giving it a little twitch, which sends out rings on the water and makes it look even more like the natural object.

bit of slack line out onto the river. This allows a few vital seconds before the current begins to straighten it out and pull the fly off course. You can also "mend" the line by lifting it up with the rod tip and looping it back over the quick current so that it is laid down again without the current-induced bow.

Spotting the rise to your fly can be difficult—sometimes it's just a dimple and nothing more. Remember that you will see the fly better against a shaded surface than a bright one, so if you can put it down under a tree you stand a better chance with delicate fish.

The fly has gone. You have to strike, but when and how? One golden rule is never to strike wildly, but simply lift the rod in a calm, controlled fashion. That's easy enough to master—it's the timing that's the problem. Generally, a quicker strike is called for in fast water. Smaller fish, too, demand an almost instant response. However, if you're tackling larger fish in slower water, especially with bigger flies, then it pays to take your time. Count to one and strike. Missed? On the next rise, count to two. If you still have no success, try counting to three next time round. That could be it, but there are no hard and fast rules. Just keep persevering until you find what's right on the day.

◄ THE FLYING DUTCHMAN
Leo is one of the very finest nymph fishermen I have ever seen at work. If ever angling were to become a spectator sport, then it would be down to Leo's grace and movement. He combines intense concentration with an almost supernatural reading of the water. He's always in total contact with his fly and always fishes with a strike indicator—a tool he calls his leveller. He understands it's imperative to know exactly the depth his nymphs are fishing.

The Upstream Nymph

Fishing the upstream nymph is a lovely way of tackling a river, especially for trout. You don't need to be seeing rises to know that you're fishing effectively, because you're targeting trout beneath the surface that are taking food close to the bottom, around weed beds and in among stones. One of the great skills of upstream nymphing is finding the fish, either by spotting trout deep down or by working out where they are likely to be lying. You need to think how the current is working, where food could be pushed along and where the fish might take up good vantage and ambush points. Again, don't rush to fish, but sit and take your time and watch intently. Gradually, the river will begin to talk to you and suggest its own options.

So you think you've seen a trout, perhaps 3 or 4 feet down, feeding comparatively energetically. You now have to consider which nymph to use and where to place it so that it's at the right level in the water when it gets into the zone of the feeding fish. If you put on too heavy a fly and cast it too far upstream, then it will simply hit bottom and stick there. If you put on too light a fly and don't cast it far enough above the feeding trout, then it will simply skate away unseen over its head. This is the key to upstream nymphing, and you've got to know

your flies. Literally test them out in the bath before you set out, or in the shallows before you fish them. It's imperative to know exactly what the sink rate of each one is so that you can fish them in the taking zone all the time—not that anyone ever achieves that level of skill, of course!

◄ ROD WORK
One very noticeable thing about Leo's style of fishing is his continuous arm movement so that the rod is always working in seemingly unconventional ways. Leo is not a purist. Style is unimportant for its own sake. What Leo concentrates on is endless, effortless control. He's a big man and he uses his length and his strength to the very best advantage. He virtually always wades—getting close to the fish is an essential part of his technique.

⅋ GLOWING COLORS
One aspect of Leo's approach is his total desire to catch. He fishes with an intensity and a hunger that almost guarantees him success. Mind you, he totally appreciates the caliber of the fish that he catches, and who could fail to when you look at a grayling as fine as this?

⩕ LEO'S FISH

Yet another grayling slides toward Leo's waiting hand. The deep-fished nymph—and it can be fished at any level under a strike indicator—will pick up almost any fish that swims. Trout and grayling are obvious suckers, but so is everything from bluegill to walleye.

⩕ THE STRIKE INDICATOR

Strike indicators come in all shapes, forms, sizes, and colors. It's wise to take a whole selection with you as you're never quite sure what conditions you're going to face. Ideally, the indicator should be just buoyant enough to float the nymph or team of nymphs without sinking beneath the surface. If it rides too proudly then subtle takes can often be missed.

Having absolutely the right nymph is rarely that important, providing it's brown, green, or black in color and of a reasonable size, generally a size 10 to 14. Let's suppose you've seen fish, or you think you know where fish might be, and in goes your nymph with a slight plop. How do you know when a trout has made up its mind and sipped in your artificial? Well, often you won't know—even experts often don't know—but there are skills to develop. Grease your leader, so that you can see it lying on the water as it drifts back toward you, and if it stops or shoots forward, or even moves from side to side, strike at once. The take will sometimes be so strong that your fly line will jab upstream. Unmissable!

Of course, if the rules of the water allow it, you could use a strike indicator. This not only gives a supreme signal of a taking fish, but also allows you to select exactly the depth you want the nymph to fish at. I'll talk more about this in the next chapter, on the subject of grayling. There's no doubt that tiny blobs of polystyrene fixed onto your leader do make for easier fishing, but is it fair?

Don't neglect the importance of sight fishing when you're upstream nymphing. On many waters, in the right light conditions, you'll actually be seeing the fish that you're targeting. When you're pretty sure the nymph is in its general area, take note if it flashes forward or moves quickly from one side to the other. Does it suddenly rise up in the water? Quick movements like these should send out a positive message. If you're very lucky, you might even see the mouth open—typically there is suddenly a flash of white as the lips and inner mouth gleam. You know then, for sure, that some food item has been sucked in, and it could well be yours.

As with the dry fly, don't strike wildly. All you need do is lift your rod and tighten and the fish will be on—providing, of course, that there aren't great loops of loose line between you and your nymph. It's vitally important to keep in touch with your nymph at all times as it moves back toward you with the current. This means practiced hand-to-eye co-ordination. You've got to strip line back at the same rate that it's drifting along with the current: too slow, and you'll end up with slack; too fast, and you'll be pulling the nymph upward, unnaturally, through the water.

➤ DIBBLING
Don't be in too great a hurry to remove your fly at the end of the cast. Very frequently fish—salmon especially—will follow a fly with great curiosity for many yards while deciding whether or not to take. It often pays to just dibble your fly for a few seconds before removing it to cast again. Takes at short range are frequently strong and sudden, so be ready to give line quickly to a hard-running fish.

rod held high

tight line to nymphs

watch for line movements to indicate a take

use of an indicator can help detect bites

◄ NYMPH FISHING
Nymph fishing is an art form: you have to choose the right pattern, fish it at the right depth, in the right place, and at the right speed to a taking fish. Keep very close contact with your nymph all the time, so you have a focused idea of where it's operating, and make sure the nymph drifts as naturally as possible down to the waiting fish. You also have to detect the take, which can be very gentle. Polarizing glasses will help you see as much of the action as possible. You can strike on a hunch—perhaps the white gash of a mouth opening or the trout moving unexpectedly from its lie in the water.

Czech Nymphing

As it's name suggests, this style of nymphing was principally developed in central-eastern Europe in the Czech Republic, Slovakia, and, to a degree, in Poland. These are places, or at least they were until recently, where successful fishing was essential to put food on the table. Czech nymphing was developed to fish the nymph as effectively as possible, and it's a very effective technique on virtually any river, no matter what its size or flow.

There are certain basic essentials. Firstly, you're almost certainly going to have to wade, because the whole key to Czech nymphing is getting very close indeed to your fish. In fact, you're hardly casting at all. You also need a slightly longer than average rod—10 feet is about perfect. The next consideration is that you will almost certainly be

▼ ROD POSITIONING
Another shot of Franta in blistering action that fascinating morning. Notice how his rod is held very high. This keeps as much fly line as possible out of the water, and this in turn gives him greater control over the movement of his nymphs beneath the surface. Bites are very rapid and often extremely gentle. He'll be watching that length of fly line, and if it straightens momentarily then almost certainly there will be a fish on.

using a strike indicator. You'll rarely be using one fly, but rather two or three. The diagram below explains the setup, but the general idea is for a heavier nymph to bounce along the bottom with either one or two slightly lighter nymphs working a few inches off it.

This means that you've got to know exactly how the nymphs work in the water, and the Czechs themselves spend endless amounts of time not only tying nymphs, but also watching how they behave. You need to know the sink rate of each one and how it rides in the current, and it must look as natural as possible. This is a strongly imitative type of fishing, and the nymphs are tied to represent shrimp, caddis grubs, or small beetles. The target fish for the Czechs themselves are nearly always trout and grayling, and you'll find that the flies are generally tied on size 12 or 14 to merge in exactly with the usual food on the drift downstream.

The technique is to look for a stretch of steadily paced water

between 4 and 7 feet deep and to wade out as far as you can, so that you've only got to cast a maximum of 3 or 4 yards. The strike indicator is set on the leader at such a depth that the heaviest fly is just bouncing down along the bottom, so you're

⋏ HOOKED
It's very instructive to watch grayling taking flies—either imitative or real—in the water. You'd be amazed at the speed with which they can suck in and spit out, and a few minutes of study will soon help you to realize why a strike indicator is such an essential element of grayling fishing.

➢ CZECH NYMPHING
One of the basics of this technique is presenting a team of two or even three nymphs close to the riverbed and making them work in as natural a way as possible. One heavy nymph will keep the team down in the critical area while the lighter ones will skip and work up to a foot from the bottom. Sensing the take is critical to any nymphing technique, so use your powers of touch and sight to their utmost.

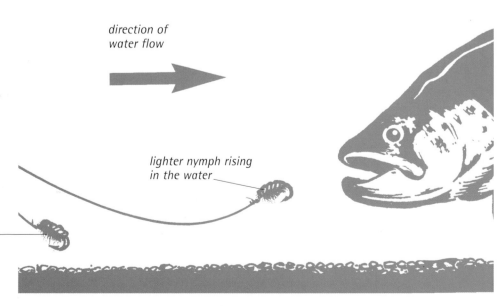

direction of water flow

lighter nymph rising in the water

heavily weighted nymph fished close to the bottom

hoping the run in front of you will be fairly clean sand or gravel. You begin by flicking your leader, with its three flies and strike indicator, out and upstream of you at an angle of about 45 degrees to the current. Keep your rod high so that there is little, if any, fly line on the water and you're direct to the strike indicator. As the current pushes your rig downstream, follow it with the rod tip, keeping that direct contact. When the current takes your gear downstream of you, begin to lower your rod tip to give yourself another yard or so of fishing time. When you can let the strike indicator go no further, simply draw it out and, perhaps with a roll cast, flick it back to where you began in the first place.

What are you looking for? A lot depends on the species, but generally that strike indicator will hold up, zip upstream, move from side to side, or dip under. If it does anything untoward, strike. If you don't get any action after five or six casts, then take a pace or two downstream and fish the next piece of water.

This really is an effective method. In Mongolia a couple of years ago, two expert English anglers were grayling fishing an eddy just off a major river. They were taking a good-sized grayling about every 10 minutes. Radim, an expert Czech nymph fisherman, asked if he could have a few minutes in the water there and they readily agreed. He swung his Czech nymph into action and, quite literally, landed 50 grayling in 50 casts.

➢ ON THE MOVE

Here, I'm grayling fishing in the very late autumn and I'm on a roll. I've found a big shoal of fish but they're jittery and, although they're willing to take, they keep on the move. I've got to go with them, laying down a cast, taking a fish, playing it, returning it, and then catching up with the group.

⋏ NYMPHING IN LATE SUMMER

Stan and Mindy are on a river that is crystal clear, heavily weeded, and full of very shy fish. Stan is a great pursuer of sighted fish, and Mindy, with her background of bonefish sport in the Caribbean, won't take much teaching. Stan's technique is to cover the water quietly but quickly, keeping natural vegetation between him and the fish that he is pursuing. He'll be looking for a good fish—either big or beautifully conditioned—and one that's feeding. Once he's decided on a target, he'll take his time, approach very carefully, and work out a top strategy.

➢ SMOKING RIVER

The river at dawn, pewter, racing, and full of promise. Very often you will find fish of all species in the fast water at the very start of the day. They've pushed up into the rapids during the hours of darkness. Night has lent them security in the shallow water and they know that there are rich food stocks there.

Traditional Wet Fly Fishing

In general terms, a nymph is meant to imitate items of a fish's food as exactly as possible. A more traditional wet fly will try to "deceive" fish into thinking that it is natural, but it's more an impression than an exact imitation. Flies such as the Connemara Black and the sooty olive look somewhat like insects being pushed along in the current. Other wets, such as the Dunkeld or the Silver Invicta, fall into the category of "attractors"—that is, they look a bit like food items, but they flash in the water and catch the fish's eye.

One reason these flies work is that, by and large, you're fishing them in shallow, rough, quick water, where the fish, generally a trout, doesn't have too much time to make its mind up. It sees the flies, generally likes the look of them, and makes a grab. A lot of wet fly water is on wilder, untamed rivers, often with stony or rocky bottoms. Look for quick, riffly water between 1 and 3 feet in depth. These can be ideal wading conditions, getting you to the places that shore fishing can't reach. Read the water thoughtfully, and look for the little pots and holes behind larger rocks or the creases between fast and slower water. The fish will want to conserve their energy by staying in slower water, but they will be keeping a very beady eye on the current, always ready to whip out to seize a tasty morsel.

Wet flies are fished "across and down". The cast is made at about 45 degrees downstream across the river toward the far bank. The idea is that the fly, or flies, then follow the current down, moving across it to end up on your side of the river. So far so good, but what you don't want to happen is for the current to catch the fly line and push at it, making the flies work too quickly across the current, or even causing them to skate across the surface. You must slow the fly line down to give the wets time to fish at the right depth and at the right speed, and to accomplish this you mend your line to prevent the current dragging it. It's an essential technique, so get some practice in as soon as possible.

You won't miss takes when they come—the flies are moving quickly, so the trout often have to spring to intercept them, and the result is nearly always a good old tug. You'll either feel it in the fingers or see the line tighten fast across the stream. The fish is generally self-hooked, so you needn't worry about counting to three now!

Fishing the wet fly might not have quite the finesse of the upstream nymph, but it's wildly exciting and hugely effective in the right water. It also demands a good reading of the river, and you've got to be prepared to walk, wade, and put yourself out physically if you are to get the best results.

◄ STEALTH
There are no rules about fishing tiny, overgrown streams. It's all down to stealth and cunning. Get to the water as quietly and as well hidden as you possibly can, watch the fish, and then work out a wily plan! Upstream or down it doesn't really matter. Sometimes you can simply let the line flow with the current and twitch the fly back, so no cast is actually needed. Dibble a fly under the rod tip so that no line is on the surface of the water at all, while making sure your rod is actually hidden in overhanging tree branches.

Salmon Fishing

I'm quite aware that it's impossible to give anything more than the briefest details of salmon fishing in a few hundred words, especially when you consider that there have been more books written about salmon than any other area of fly fishing. It is a huge topic that has provoked endless debate for centuries. Salmon waters themselves are endlessly disparate—they can be tiny streams, medium rivers, or roaring spring creeks. You can even catch salmon in the tidal reaches. They can be enormous—40 pounds or more—or they can be modest—just 2 or 3 pounds. If you're talking about Pacific salmon, then kings can exceed 80 pounds. In Europe, salmon fishing tends to be expensive, but in the United States and Canada, the rivers that flow to the Pacific coast offer the salmon angler unrivaled sport, as wave after wave of the various salmon species make their way upstream—chinook, sockeye, pink, coho, chum, and not forgetting the steelhead trout. Make a point of finding out when and where they are on the move, and you'll have some tremendous fishing.

BATTLE PLANS

I really like this photograph. The angler is about to fish the pool, but before he does so he takes time out to study it as carefully as he can through polarizing glasses. He's not just looking for fish, although that will help him plan an attack. He's taking mental note of the depth, drop-offs, the current speed and direction, and any large boulders that might offer sanctuary to fish. Only when he's quite sure that he has the geography of the pool committed to memory will he begin to fish—a good lesson for anyone new to a river.

Fishing Cold Waters

Cold-water salmon are probably the most difficult of the lot, but they will take a fly if it can be seen and if it is presented perfectly. When the temperatures are low, salmon live in a near torpor, unwilling to leave their secure lies, and certainly not willing to chase a fly moving quickly over their heads. It's vital, therefore, to get a visible fly right down among the fish and to move it slowly and methodically as close to their noses as possible. A boat can be useful in these circumstances, as it puts the fisherman in the very best position to present a fly with precision in a known taking area.

Generally speaking, a medium-sink, double-taper fly line is the perfect starter for cold conditions, although a fast-sink line can play its part in very deep, dark pools when the fish are stubbornly remaining on the bottom. It's tempting to go for big rods and heavy lines, but the angler mustn't over-rod himself and lose control of his tackle, especially if there's a strong wind about. A 14- or 15-foot rod is about right, even for a larger river, but it's sensible to go shorter if the pools are more intimate.

Fly choice is all-important in cold water early in the season, and it's vital that whatever is used makes a strong impression. If the fish are lying half frozen in deep water, their reactions will be much slower than those of summer fish, and they will not be willing to come to the surface to chase flies across a pool. A 2- to 3-inch tube fly is about right for a medium to large river, and preferably a fly with bright, attention-grabbing colors such as hot orange, red, yellow, and black.

It's really important to visualize what the fly's movements are in the pool, to work it, to instill life into it, and yet to make sure that it is searching every possible salmon-holding lie as thoroughly as possible. In icy conditions, when the water itself is dead and dour, the fly has to practically tap a salmon on the nose before a take is induced. Even then, after a slow, gentle draw on the line as the fish rises slightly from the bottom, the salmon may well sink back down to sanctuary behind a boulder once again, refusing to take.

⅄ AT THE FALLS

Waterfalls are productive places to fish. In hot conditions the oxygen count rises dramatically. Perhaps even more importantly, the tumble of water cascading into a pool gives off a barrage of sound, sufficient to mask the approach of the angler and the lay of his line. Always remember that sound travels five times as far under water as it does above, so the noise of even a light nymph landing in a placid stream is instantly registered.

Summer Fishing

Conditions can be easier in the summer when the water is warmer, lower and clearer and the fish are more actively on the move. Then you can generally fish shorter rods – anything between 10 and 12 feet – and almost always with a floating line. This is the cream of the sport.

It's probably best to go for a double-tapered line, but match the leader with the fly, the size of the fish, and the power of the water. A small fly on a heavy leader does not fish well, and breaking strains of about 8 or 10 pounds are about right. It's important that the fly doesn't skate across the river, but actually sinks about 6 inches below the surface. A multi-hooked fly is more difficult to sink than a single-hooked fly, as its extra bulk causes more drag in the water. Equally, a sparsely dressed single-hooked fly

may sink faster and truer than one that is over elaborate. Moving to a slightly larger hook, say from an 8 to a 6, might also give a bit of extra weight. It's also worthwhile sinking the leader if you think it's necessary.

Even in the best conditions and when the river is full of salmon, the fly must be fished intelligently. If the water is very still, then a cast across the river can be made and the fly can be worked back by hand. If there's a brisk current, however, then it's important to cast well downstream and let the fly hang over the most likely water. It's also a good idea to hold the rod at right angles to the flow of the river, so that the slowest possible fly speed across the current is achieved. Lastly, it can be vital in a fast current to mend the line and prevent a large loop being formed, which would allow the current to pull the fly quickly off course.

▲ THE TREE FRINGE
It doesn't matter what species of fish you are pursuing, overhanging trees are of vital importance to them. Trout and bass, for example, will look for the tree fringes not only for shade but also for the continual dropping of terrestrial insects, such as moths, wasps, and caterpillars. Salmon—the species being fished here—also seek the shadow and security that branches bring as they journey upriver.

The hotter the weather becomes and the longer the fish have been in the river, the more "stale" they become and the more difficult they are to tempt. They've probably seen several anglers by now, too, and they're getting used to fly lines and flies. Seek out new pools and fish that haven't been repeatedly covered. Try to fish after rain, when oxygen has been pumped into the water and there might be a tinge of color. An extra flow will also make the fly work in a more sprightly fashion.

Indeed, if conditions are really hard and the water is really low and bright, then a tiny fly might make all the difference—even a single-hooked black fly, no bigger than a size 12 or 14.

⍦ SALMON FISHING

Before you fish a salmon pool take as long as it needs to work out exactly what's happening. Don't just begin to thrash the water, rather formulate a plan of attack. Consider the direction and speed of the current. Try to gauge how deep the pool is. Endeavor to find out whereabouts the salmon are lying and how deep you need to fish your fly. Look for salmon in midwater or even coming to the surface. If you see this then a floating line is going to be all you need. Otherwise you might have to go deep with a sinker. In particular, look for rocks and underwater obstructions that give the salmon a little protection from the main flow of the water. Start at the head of the pool and work your way slowly down, covering the water as thoroughly as you can manage. Concentrate all the time. Takes can be very gentle.

Work down the pools methodically with total control. Cast a couple of times from each stance, and then drop two paces downriver before casting again. Put the fly across the river and slightly downstream, and let it work across in a steady movement. Really concentrate as the fly swings around in the current because there are critical taking points. Don't expect big bangs… you'll probably get a gentle tightening of the line and nothing more. Don't strike frenziedly, but just lift into the fish. It's one of the wonders of fly fishing when you lift that rod, see the surface boil, and hear your reel begin to shriek.

ROCKS

Rocks are a major part of the salmon's life in the river, and they shelter around them for large periods of time. Drift your flies as close to the rock as you can and always try to hold it for a short period in the dead water behind.

Spring Creeks

One of the most exciting (and often cheapest) openings for salmon is on the small spring creek. These are often wild waters, no more than 20 or 30 yards across. They rise in uplands and have comparatively short, steep descents to the sea. Heavy rain makes them flood quickly, and salmon waiting to ascend will bolt up toward the spawning redds in great numbers. The key is to be in close contact with the weather and water conditions. You need to be on the river the instant it begins

RAPIDS

Salmon will run up the rapids, often at night, into the next pool. They'll often rest for quite a while once they've done this, so always concentrate hard on the tail of a pool. If the rapid isn't too deep and swift, it's often a good idea to fish from it. You will find that you're more directly in line with the fish below you and the line needs to be mended less.

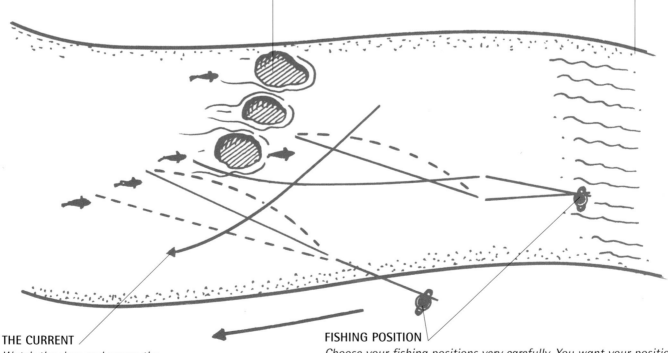

THE CURRENT
Watch the river and gauge the current speed both in the margin and in the middle. The water is going to be faster on the surface than down on the bottom.

FISHING POSITION
Choose your fishing positions very carefully. You want your position to give you the best possible opportunity of placing the fly close to the fish. If you see a number of fish, try to pick off the fish that is least likely to alarm the others. For example, in this diagram you could possibly hook the salmon that's lying furthest away and then let it run downstream, out of the vision of the others.

to drop and fine down. Timing is absolutely critical. Leave it a day too late, and the fish have already gone upstream and are uncatchable. Hit it exactly right and you can have the salmon fishing of your life.

Slightly stepped-up trout gear will often be fine for fishing on waters like this. A 9- or 10-foot rod, a floating line, and a leader of 6 or 8 pounds is often all you'll need. If the water is colored, use orange or black flies about an inch long. However, if you're not catching fish but you're pretty sure they are about, then change color, change size, and keep experimenting until you unlock that door.

This is very hands-on, active, close-up fishing. Travel light and be prepared to walk miles, often through very rough terrain. Look at all the little pools, gullies, and holding areas,

and make up your mind exactly where the fish are likely to be lying and how best to approach them. As so often, it's all about patience and choosing the right strategy.

Chest waders will be essential so you can get in the river and put your fly exactly where you want it, whether that be under fallen trees or behind a rock. Tightness of control is everything. You'll need to be able to make accurate, short casts in the most overhung of conditions. This is the place for the roll cast or the steeple cast. Sometimes you will simply let your line float with the current to the desired spot and then work the fly back. Don't hesitate to hang your fly in the current and let it dibble around a good area for a minute or more. Impart real life into the fly so that it looks like a darting fish, sufficiently realistic to arouse

▽ LOW WATER
Low conditions in summer almost always make for difficult fishing. The salmon will be holed up, often in deep pools under snags and overhanging trees, totally disinclined to feed. They may travel at night. If they're going to be caught then it's frequently either down deep or in areas of running water like this that give a bit of life and vigor to the fly. Dawn and dusk are probably the best times to be out in the hope of catching a moving fish. Alternatively, wait for heavy summer rainstorms, colored, rising water, and fish on the move once more.

◀ MAKING A STATEMENT
In quick, white water you often need a large fly that is immediately visible and makes a real statement to the fish. A big fly like this flowing past in the current won't be inspected minutely but grabbed because it resembles a living creature. Often color can be important. For example, if fish have been feeding on shrimp out at sea, a big orange fly can trigger an instant reaction.

The Challenge of Steelhead

Just like the salmon, the steelhead is a magnificent creature, and countless anglers have devoted their entire lives to its capture. So, what I have to say now is only the briefest run through the rules regarding this spellbinding creature. Steelhead fishing doesn't get better than in British Columbia, but you've got to time your visit accurately because the windows of opportunity are fairly narrow. For example, on the Skeena/Babine system, September, October, and early November are really favored. In September the water is still warm and most of the fishing takes place on the surface with floating flies. October sees more fish moving upstream and you're still fishing comparatively shallow, but possibly now with a sink-tip line.

the salmon's anger or curiosity. Impart life by working your rod tip, moving it up and down and from side to side, especially in slow water where you just can't rely on the current to do the job for you. You'll also have to master the "mending" of the line, or your fly will constantly be pulled off course into the margins where the water is dead and useless.

Fish all these small pools and runs quickly, accurately, and with supreme concentration. Don't spend too long in a place if you're not catching fish, or where you have no indication there are fish. Always be watching for salmon—you might well see them splash out of the water, but more often you will just see them glint, even in quite tainted water, if the sun is shining.

In these conditions, you're fishing for salmon that are always on the move, so you'll only get short, sharp openings of possibility before the fish leave the pool and are on their way again.

It's always very tempting to fish the quicker, more active water, but a

good number of salmon will lie up in slow, seemingly dead stretches. Look for them lying inert in shade, particularly under overhanging branches. They might be lying in the slacker water behind rocks. Wherever they are, it's up to you to find them, put a fly in front of their noses, and work it back in an intriguing fashion.

Don't be too quick to strike, especially in slow water. Wait until the fly line begins to move off before lifting your rod. This is very important in all salmon fly fishing— a lot of salmon are missed simply by striking as soon as the take is registered. This works in really fast water where the fish virtually hooks itself, but where the water is slower always give it time.

▼ FRY FEEDERS
Look how these flies are tied to imitate small fish. They've even got tiny eyes for the predators to target in on. In the water these flies realistically twist and flutter in the current. Flies like this are taken by big trout, steelhead, taimen, pike, salmon... virtually anything big enough to consume them!

October is a great month as the cool nights clear the water perfectly. In late October and early November you find the big, trophy fish on the move. The weather has cooled down appreciably, and sometimes you need to fish your fly more deeply in the water—although big, surface-skating flies can take fish even in snowstorms.

For steelhead, try a 9- or 10-foot 8-weight rod, or a single-handed salmon rod. Keep with your floating line as long as possible and try large, surface-working flies, such as the Muddler Minnow. You can even add on extra bristles to make it skate more noticeably across the surface. This is especially exciting fishing, and you'll often see steelhead powering into the fly as it drags across the current. For general flies, the larger versions of European reservoir lures in various colors are excellent. Local fishermen often tie

flies that are made to look like the salmon eggs upon which the steelheads feed.

If you've taken this chapter in, you are unlikely to be out of your depth when it comes to steelhead fishing—until, that is, you hook one! Nothing, in my experience, fights better on a fly rod than a fresh-run steelhead. Those first 30 seconds often seem as though the fish is moving violently in every direction at once, and it's easy to lose your head totally, to panic, to let the reel overrun, to let tangles stack up, and to lose the fish. Hang on, though. Keep a clear head, and wait for the initial ferocity of the fight to die down a little.

As you can imagine, you need to be sure that your tackle is absolutely perfect for this job. There's no tolerance here. It's all raw, white-knuckle stuff. Check your leader for any abrasions, double-check all knots, and make sure that the hook

⋀ KEEPING IT TIGHT
Whether you're fighting a big fish or a small fish it's essential to keep the line tight to it. If you give a fish slack, a hook, especially a barbless one, can come away instantly.

of the fly hasn't been blunted on rocks. Ensure, too, that the drag of your reel is set at exactly the right tension—not too slack and not too stiff. Always fish comfortably, making sure that you are well balanced—in the event of a smashed take you don't want to go headlong into a freezing river.

Oh, and be careful of bears, both grizzlies and blacks. If they're on a pool before you it's good manners and good sense to move on. If they fancy fishing a pool that you're already on, then forget etiquette and clear off fast! I speak as one who had a juvenile grizzly chase after him for a full 20 yards, and it's not an experience I'd care to repeat.

ISLANDS

Islands are important because they check the flow of the river, and you'll find fish sheltering in the calm water downstream of them. Migratory fish, in particular, look for this type of slack water.

FEEDER STREAMS

Feeder streams will always hold a stock of resident fish that may be small but that are fun to catch. They're also frequently investigated by bigger fish either looking to spawn or looking for an easy meal.

EDDIES

On any large river you'll find bits of water where the current just swirls around and around in an apparently aimless fashion. Eddies aren't generally very good during normal water conditions, but when the river is really up and flowing, many fish will push into them looking for refuge. Try a large, colorful fly.

BRIDGES

No fisherman in his right mind can ever pass a bridge without stopping and looking over. Bridges give perfect vantage points, and bridge pools are historically famous for holding fish. The currents created by the parapets generally deepen out the riverbed and form succulent pools.

Big Rivers

Big rivers just steam along and, when they get to being a football field wide, can look hugely intimidating. Don't be frightened, however. Take time to work out their features and everything will fall into place. Wading a river is often a huge advantage to the fly fisherman but be wary of fast currents or deep drop-offs. Don't wade unless the water is clear, you're wearing polarizing glasses and, preferably, you've got a wading stick and a flotation device.

Big rivers can offer a wide range of fish species. You'll probably have resident fish like trout, grayling, or even pike. But you can also expect to come across migratory fish like salmon, cutthroat trout, and steelhead. Look for the bigger fish, like running salmon, out in the main body of the water. However, you'll find smaller fish, perhaps modest trout or grayling, a little closer into the margins where the current is less pushy and where they feel safe from predators.

Big rivers the world over offer a wildly exciting challenge, and if you can catch them in good shape you will enjoy the fishing experience of your life. Don't be too worried if conditions aren't kind to you, for example, if the water is unusually high. You'll be surprised how many fish you can pick up in slower water close to the bank providing you use large, colorful, highly visible flies. Always fish in hope and you may surprise yourself.

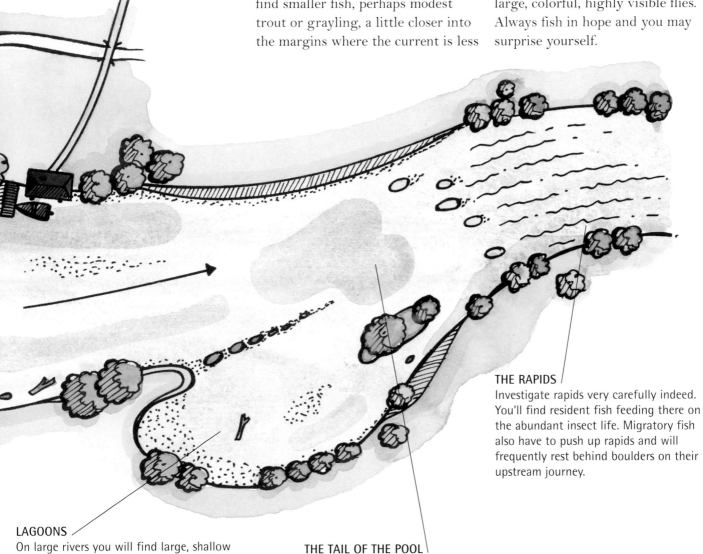

THE RAPIDS
Investigate rapids very carefully indeed. You'll find resident fish feeding there on the abundant insect life. Migratory fish also have to push up rapids and will frequently rest behind boulders on their upstream journey.

LAGOONS
On large rivers you will find large, shallow lagoons where there is hardly any flow at all. These generally only harbor small fish, but come dusk big fish move in for the kill.

THE TAIL OF THE POOL
The tail of the pool is a critical area. Fish that are tired from the rapids enter the pool and rest up almost immediately. Also, the water is frequently comparatively shallow, so presenting the fly at the right depth isn't quite as critical as it is in the main body of the pool where the depth increases.

ROCKY SHALLOWS
At dawn and dusk, trout and grayling will come onto rocky shallows knowing that there will be a feast of nymphs, shrimp, and snails. Approach them carefully.

TREES
Terrestrial food items are very important in small rivers. You'll find smaller fish, in particular, always hovering under tree branches, safe from kingfishers and other predators.

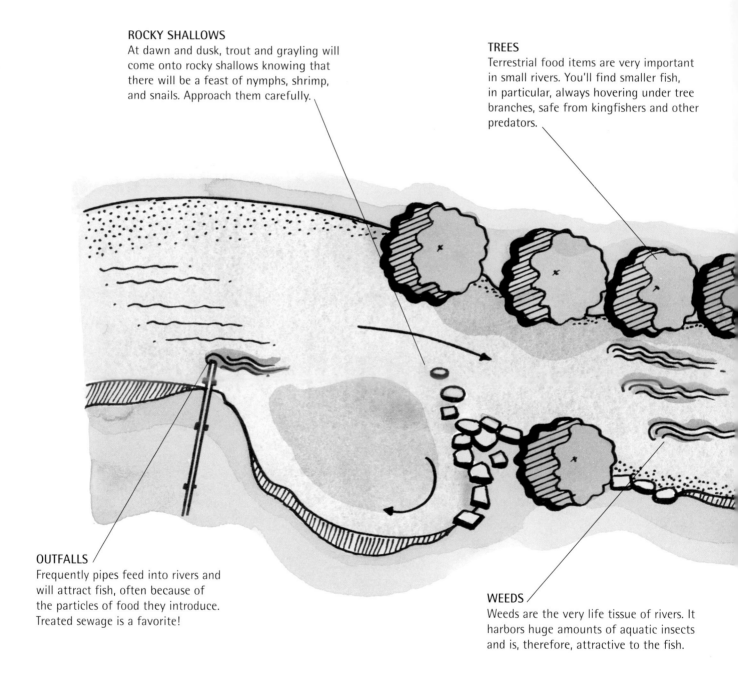

OUTFALLS
Frequently pipes feed into rivers and will attract fish, often because of the particles of food they introduce. Treated sewage is a favorite!

WEEDS
Weeds are the very life tissue of rivers. It harbors huge amounts of aquatic insects and is, therefore, attractive to the fish.

Small Rivers

Fishing a small, clear river can be one of the most satisfying experiences in the fly-fisher's life. If the water is clear and prolific you will see a huge amount of fly life and, probably, different types of feeding activity. There's also something terribly intimate about the atmosphere of a small river and you can grow to love them in a way that you can't much larger waters.

Anglers will often fish their local small rivers a hundred times a year throughout a lifetime and never once get bored. They're always changing after every winter flood and big, resident, wild fish can present an individual challenge year upon year. On large rivers you don't always see the fish so you can't always tell if you are doing things right or wrong. On small rivers, however, the fish are nearly always clearly in view and if

you're not catching, then you're making mistakes.

Some of the most difficult fly-fishing challenges take place on small, crystal-clear rivers that are immensely rich in fly life. Here, the fish are supremely sophisticated and, being well fed, need not take any risks. Also, the chances are, they've seen every angling trick in the book and it will take something very special to wheedle them out.

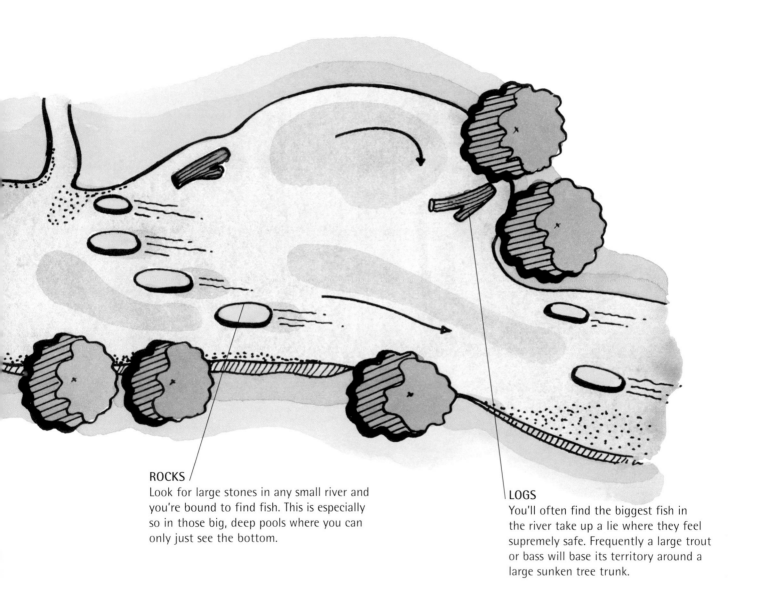

ROCKS
Look for large stones in any small river and you're bound to find fish. This is especially so in those big, deep pools where you can only just see the bottom.

LOGS
You'll often find the biggest fish in the river take up a lie where they feel supremely safe. Frequently a large trout or bass will base its territory around a large sunken tree trunk.

TOTAL FLY FISHING

ONE OF THE MOST EXCITING DEVELOPMENTS IN THE WORLD OF
FLY FISHING, AND ONE THAT HAS HAPPENED ALMOST WITHOUT
US KNOWING IT OVER THE LAST 20 OR 30 YEARS, IS THAT NOW
VIRTUALLY EVERY FISH THAT SWIMS CAN BE TARGETED ON THE FLY.
TROUT AND SALMON WERE ONCE CONSIDERED THE EXCLUSIVE
TARGETS, BUT NOW EVEN SHARKS CAN BE FLY FISHED.

Nothing is beyond the limit of our dreams. In part, of course, this is due to the extraordinary technical advances in rods, reels, lines, leaders, and flies over the period we're discussing, but hand in hand with the technical has gone the technique. Pioneers have pushed the boundaries to barely believable limits.

Perhaps we shouldn't be surprised. After all, there is virtually nothing edible that a fly can't be made to imitate, even if it has to be tied in fluorescent neon colors and is 8 inches long! It's all truly exciting, and it means that there are challenges awaiting you that your grandfather, even your father, could never have envisaged.

Bonefish on the Flats

You're never going to catch cod on a fly from a freezing beach in the middle of the night in a winter storm, but the calm days of summer, when the water is kind and clear, are quite different, and saltwater fly fishing has a lot to offer. Seashore fly fishing was really pioneered just after the Second World War around the Keys of Florida, the Bahamas, and other benevolent places. One of the main targets then, as now, was the bonefish and, to put it simply, if you're an avid

◁ BONE ISLAND
Bonefish look as though they have been fashioned out of crystal, so delicate and iridescent are their flanks. Perhaps it's the clarity of the water or the brightness of the light that paints them with this sheen of magic, but if you haven't caught one then you simply must. Precisely how a 4-pound fish can break a 10-pound tippet is beyond me, but believe me it can happen with sickening regularity. This particular fish was interesting in so far as it was caught just a matter of inches from the bank with the line actually lying on the beach itself!

➢ FEARSOME
My guide was distinctly unhappy when I put down my fly rod, picked up a spinning outfit, and cast out for this medium-sized barracuda that I saw cruising just 20 or 30 yards away from the skiff. There are those that don't sing the praise of 'cuda and, certainly, once in the boat they can create havoc. However, that first run is something to savor—on fly tackle especially. However, never forget to use a wire trace or you'll stand no chance of landing your fish.

fisherman and you haven't fished for bonefish, then put it right at the top of your "Must Do" list. The faltering steps taken half a century ago are now a confident quick trot—you can go to any one of scores of bonefish destinations around the world and be assured of magnificent sport. What should you bear in mind?

Always start with a local guide. You'll find that fishing for bonefish is like nothing else you've tried. Not only do you need to know the "flats" (vast areas of little more than ankle-deep water) where the bonefish reside, but you need to know all about the tides, currents, food sources, weed make up, and a hundred other pieces of this puzzle. You'll need to learn to use your eyes as quickly as you can, too, for this is thrilling sight fishing, and you should hone your casting before making the

journey. It's often imperative to put 25 yards of line out in an instant with barely any false casting.

Always ensure you've got the right gear before going on a major journey like this. The chances are you'll be a flight from the nearest tackle shop when you get there, so putting the matter right then is not an option.

There's a good deal of bonefish literature and you should believe what you read. Once you've hooked a bonefish there's simply no stopping it. Until I hooked my first bone, I wouldn't have believed that a 3-pound fish could strip 100 yards of line off me. These are the most electrifying fish you'll ever find, quite capable of accelerating to well over 20 miles an hour.

Question your guides intently about where they are taking you and why. You'll never be proficient, let alone as skilled as they are, but it's all part of the angling process to know exactly why you are fishing the way you are. Try to build some picture in your mind of how the bonefish react to different times of the day, weather and water conditions, and changes in terrain. You'll find everything about them utterly fascinating.

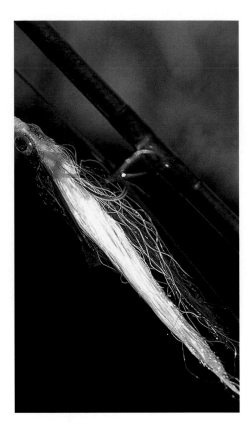

➢ STREAMER FLIES
Big, flowing flies like this work well in any current and look great when retrieved fairly quickly. They're obviously meant to represent any generic small fish and, as a result, they're taken eagerly by any predators. Striped bass love them, as does mackerel, and who knows, you might even pick up a wayward salmon.

TIPS FOR THE TRAVELING ANGLER

• Check out the new generation of multi-piece rods that break into four or five sections and can be fitted into a suitcase. They invariably have a brilliant action and there's no more struggling with rod tubes.

• Always check out the vaccinations that you need for foreign countries.

• It's always a good idea to take a couple of spare passport photographs of yourself for unexpected visas or bureaucratic demands.

• Remember that the modern lightweight materials are a breeze to wash, so you can cut down on the amount of clothing you lug about.

• Remember that out in the wilds there won't be any tackle shops, so take everything that you think you could possibly begin to need.

• Buy the very best gear that you can if you're going to travel. You get what you pay for, and substandard items are simply bound to let you down at the most critical moments.

• Vital items on the packing list include toilet paper, strong tape to wrap around a flashlight so that you can hold it in your teeth, sharp scissors, and a whistle. A good strong money belt is also invaluable.

• If you're going for a long trip, it's a good idea to have a dental checkup before leaving. Always pack a small vial of clove oil, as this could save you some sleepless nights.

• Wherever you're traveling, try to get plenty of small bills. You'll find changing money with taxi drivers in a country where you can't speak the language very difficult indeed!

• Always pack Deet and a head net—even if the guidebooks say there are no mosquitoes and you won't need them.

• In hot climates, drink 2 gallons of water—not beer—a day. If you're in any doubt over the water even clean your teeth with bottled water.

• Make it a habit to turn over your boots every morning before putting them on. You don't know what creepy-crawly might have crept into them during the night.

• Always be patient. There is no point getting stressed at airports or fuming over unexpected floods. Save your energies for things that you can actually influence.

• Even if you feel wet, cold, and defeated, don't moan. You might be crying inside but you owe it to yourself and your group to put on a brave face.

Closer to Home

Mind you, there's plenty of extraordinary sea fishing available for the fly angler without heading off to exotic destinations. Around the Atlantic coast, for example, more and more anglers are using the fly for bass and bluefish. Ideally you need spells of settled weather, preferably with winds off shore so the seas are not too stirred up. Look for fish tailing in shallow lagoons. Once hooked, you'll find they come close to the bonefish in terms of speed and athleticism.

If it's bass you're after then silvery flies a couple of inches long and set to imitate a sand eel or elver do well. Wrecks, boulders, beds of kelp, close-in depressions, tidal ribs, estuaries,

harbors… explore them all.

One of my favorites is the mackerel, a grossly underestimated species, possibly because it is so often caught and simply winched in to be eaten or used as bait. Hook one mackerel and the experience will live with you forever.

⅄ THE SEASHORE SPRINTER
There's hardly any fish around the Atlantic coastline that fights harder than a mackerel. Even a 1-pound fish will have your reel smoking. Fish for them with fry imitations, streamers, or anything that's garish and makes its presence felt.

Sea Trout

The sea trout—the sea-run brown—is really one of the icon species of our sporting world, and it's traditionally fished for when it has left the sea and entered fresh water on its way up to spawn. Sea-trout fishing is an internationally studied science, and the species is an absolute favorite for many, but fishing for sea trout in the sea itself is a relatively recent development.

The open beaches are difficult, but the estuaries are much more accessible. A great amount of work has been done in Ireland, where it has been found that the hours before and after low water can be particularly productive. My own coastal sea-trout fishing has generally been around the Scottish Isles, where ebb tides have been particularly kind to me. If you can

fish on foot, as it were, do so, because sea trout can be very nervous about boats. Don't go too light—some of the fish can be big, and you'll often need to put out fairly long casts in winds that can be sneaky in the extreme. Go for flies that imitate small fish, sand eels, prawns, and shrimp. Keep your eyes open for fish splashing on the surface after prey or perhaps fleeing from a sea otter.

Fly Casting for Pike

Pike on fly is one of the big new trends in fishing. Of course, they have been pursued on fly for innumerable years, but not with anything like the intensity of today, largely because we now have exactly the gear to do it. Don't go too light—you need heavy stuff to drive a big pike fly on a wire trace out into anything like a breeze. There's a lot

⋏ THE RIVER MOUTH
Traditionally, sea trout are fished for well upriver in fresh water, but there's a big move afoot to hunt for them where the rivers meet the sea. These are wonderful, shifting places where the tide makes a huge impact on the fishing possibilities. Local knowledge is absolutely essential, and make sure that you know exactly what is happening to the tides.

➢ EXPOSURE
This was one of the bleakest fly-fishing situations I've ever endured—howling winds, pelting rain and endless mud flats. However, the sight of legions of sea trout cartwheeling their way through the leaden waters lifted the spirits. Takes were surprisingly gentle, however, and most fish were either missed or came off after one or two somersaulting leaps.

of purpose-built stuff now in the 9- or even 10-weight category, and it pays to use it, for reasons of both efficiency and safety.

I've caught a lot of pike on fly now myself, and I would say this to beginners: start your pike fly fishing in warm weather when the fish are more active and more on the prowl, and choose small, clear-water lakes with large pike populations. This way you can build up your experience, your confidence, and your knowledge of when things are going right and wrong.

Fish the fly exactly where you would use lures or dead baits: in the shallows; around reed beds; close to lilies; under overhanging trees; close to streams, fallen trees, dumped machinery, and any other feature that's likely to bring pike in.

Be willing to change your flies quite frequently—with pike, it's not just the way that you fish the fly that's important. Use silvery flies tipped with red if there are a lot of shiners in the water. Try barred flies if you think the fish are feeding on small perch. Use very gaudy flies if the water is at all tinged.

Always use a wire trace and try to unhook the pike without taking it from the water if you possibly can.

In clear, shallow water on a bright day it is often possible to watch the reaction of the pike to the fly. Sometimes it will be ignored altogether, sometimes slowly followed and rejected, and at other times pounced upon. Experience suggests that if a pike is showing any interest at all, then it can probably be tempted by one pattern or another. Keep

◁ PREDATOR SUCCESS
A good pike on the fly is a heart-warming challenge. A fish that might not fight particularly well on beefed-up gear really gives an account of itself on a 7- or 8-weight outfit.

⌃ A CLOSER LOOK
Once again a photographer was present and, while under normal circumstance I would have simply slipped the hook, it was decided a closer examination of this very fine pike was required. And pike are beautiful. Don't be prejudiced against them. Judge all fish on their merits.

➢ THE HERO
No, I don't like hero shots any more than you do, but at least I'm holding the pike carefully and over water, so if it should drop it wouldn't be harmed in any way. Don't miss out on the thrill of fly fishing for any species. You might be a confirmed trout or salmon angler and I can understand that but, believe me, you're not doing yourself any favors if you cut yourself off from the whole spectrum of fly-fishing possibilities.

working the fish with different lures until you find one that turns it on. Don't be afraid of retrieving the lure very close to the pike, trying to annoy it—an instinctive take is often the response.

A surface lure is well worth trying, and there's nothing, absolutely nothing, more exciting in fly fishing. There are endless mouse and frog patterns available, and these should be worked back across the surface, making a really big ripple in the process. It's a technique that has worked particularly well for me in Mongolia in search of the landlocked salmon species there, the taimen, and it's heart-stopping stuff. Taimen and pike are very similar—both enormous, confident predators at the top of their respective food chains. If they do differ, it's possibly

that taimen are even more fixated on surface-swimming prey than pike. Although pike are not averse to taking the odd duckling, rat, or busily paddling frog, taimen are always actively on the lookout for lemmings and desert mice crossing their huge rivers. They're easy meat, and the taimen hammer into a surface-fished lure as though their lives depended on it.

One last point about fly piking is the tremendous use float tubes can be put to. Not everyone takes to these remarkable individual flotation devices, but they give you huge flexibility and allow you to get into otherwise unfishable positions without making anything like the commotion of a boat. If you're truly serious about your fly fishing, sooner or later you're going to have to try it.

➤ FISHING THE MOUSE
One of the most exciting forms of fly fishing I've ever done is with mouse patterns fished on the surface, twitched back through reeds, rushes, or lily pads. From above, these patterns, with their long, wriggling tails, look incredibly lifelike. From below, too, they certainly rouse the instincts of any predator. This particular pike was virtually comatose until it sensed the vibrations above.

⌄ MAN AFLOAT
Float tubing, belly boating, call it what you like but it works. Take care, however, and make sure your first session or two are done under supervision. Don't go out in high winds, and be advised that until you're used to it you'll have rather sore legs for a day or two afterward.

Black Bass

Hundreds of thousands of anglers just can't be wrong—and they're not. The bass, whether large- or small-mouth, is a gem of a fish, and one of the most beguiling opponents that the fly fisherman is ever going to meet. Most of my own bassing experience has taken place in Spain, where the species was introduced during General Franco's period of power. There, bass have really taken off, arguably becoming the Spanish number one hit.

There are many books that you can ingest on the art of bassing, and they all make pretty much the same relevant points, many of which are common to all predators. Look carefully for bass wherever there is a feature to cause them to congregate. These may be natural (weed beds, reeds, bottom contours, inflowing streams, plateaus, bays, rock falls, fallen trees, and shallow, marshy

areas), or they may be manmade (boat jetties, boathouses, dam walls, water towers, and bridges).

As in all fishing, the experts pay particular attention to location, and that's largely why the top tournament fishermen have such huge and mighty motorboats enabling them to travel 50 miles, even 100 miles, up and down the great lakes during the day. On deep waters it's especially important to gauge the depth that the bass are working and feeding in, and here an electronic fish finder plays an important part. So does local knowledge, as does the state of the weather and the seasons. Just as with bonefish sport, or any other developed fishing, come to that, bass fishing is about putting all the little ingredients together and coming up with a successful solution.

Much of my bass fishing has been wildly exciting and enjoyable. But

⋏ A FASCINATING FELLOW

Black bass have it all. They're gorgeous to look at with an amazing kaleidoscope of colors along the flanks. They fight well. They can be incredibly cunning and just when you've given up on them one makes a foolish mistake and your belief in yourself as an angler is restored. Of course, they can be taken on bait and lure, but it's fly fishing that really works for me. If the water is clear and you can watch your fly and the fish's reaction to it then you're light years ahead. Frequently a bass will simply sip in a fly, hold it there for a second and then eject it. Without sight, you wouldn't even guess you'd had a take.

it's often quite hard work. On my more relaxed sorties in Spain, I've approached bass from a quieter, more intimate point of view, and my findings include the following:

• You're likely to find bass where nobody else has thought to fish for them. You'll frequently find them so close into the bank you'd hardly believe it. They are hypersensitive to any clumsy approach and can sense footsteps or boat engines huge distances away. For these reasons it pays, in my opinion, to move slowly and quietly around any water, fishing carefully and intently and keeping your eyes wide open.

• Don't give up on a fish that you might catch. I've frequently changed fly 10, 20, even 30 times, and finally caught a fish that appeared impossible to tempt.

• Don't always expect takes that are detectable through the fingers. A favorite bass trick is to ghost up to a fly, suck it in, sample it, and spit it out without any movement whatsoever. Unless you can actually see such a take you stand no chance of hitting it.

• Fishing flies along the surface so that they pop, skitter and send out "V" waves is as about as exciting as fishing comes.

• Expect your bass to move around a fair bit. Fish that I have located in the morning have frequently been hundreds of yards away come the afternoon. Just because you catch in one area one day doesn't mean to say it will be hot the next.

• Make instant use of any phenomena on your side. For example, a savage summer thunderstorm will cause the lake's feeder streams to swell and large areas of clouded water will hang at the feeder mouths. The bass go berserk there, so make for them.

• In very clear, hot weather, get out at dawn, as well as dusk. If rules allow it, try well into darkness.

• If you're on vacation and you can pick your day, don't choose the weekend. Go out in the week when the lakes are much quieter and you'll catch more fish.

• Choice of flies is a tricky one because I've caught bass on imitative nymphs, typical trout reservoir lures, and streamer flies. I've also had them on mayfly and crane-fly patterns, both twitched on the surface. Beetle patterns work well twitched along the bottom and close to weed. My advice would be to take everything and try everything until you find success. Be bold and imaginative.

▼ TO HAND
A lovely fly-caught black bass slips beaten to the margins where its mouth is held open for a second so that the fly can be slipped loose. You can see from the reflection that the day is a hot one and this bass was taken down very deep where the species goes as the heat rises. The very early morning is by far the best time to be out after this particular species.

Arctic Char

In Europe, char fishing is a freshwater business, hunting them in deep glacial lakes, where they became imprisoned at the end of the last Ice Age. However, in Greenland, the char live as they have always done, in the sea itself, ascending the rivers to spawn. Both environments offer their own attractions.

It has to be said that most freshwater char tend to be on the small side (except in central Europe) and they are generally down very, very deep where fly fishing is difficult. However, there are times when the char do render themselves vulnerable. For example, on summer evenings after hot days they will frequently come to the surface and feed in bays and shallow water. Then they can be tempted on small dry flies. In periods of very dull, wet, and windy weather, too, you will sometimes find char coming into comparatively shallow water, where they can be picked up in the 5- to 20-foot range on deep-fished nymphs. On many lakes they have well-defined spawning beds a short way up feeder rivers, and here they can be caught on big flashy flies that probably excite their territorial instincts.

The best time to hit these fish is in the autumn just as their spawning runs are beginning. They tend to run during the night, so fish for them at dusk or dawn. Look for ambush points where the spawning streams narrow and you can cover most of the water. Remember that you are just hoping to intercept fish that are highly mobile, moving rapidly upstream and then back into the main body of the lake. Be very careful with the fish at this time of the year, as even large lakes don't have endless populations of big, mature fish. Play them firmly and unhook them in the water.

> SIMPLY GLORIOUS

Sometimes you catch fish that absolutely take your breath away. You can't wrap your head around the fact that so many nature lovers are only interested in birds or mammals. Can there be any more beautiful creation on Earth than this stunning Arctic char? Look at its shape, perfectly adapted for its lifestyle, but above all just look at that coloring. Where else in nature would you see such colors?

Y EVER GLORIOUS

You can lay out a score of char, photograph them, study the results, and realize that every fish is magnificently different. The shape, the size, the coloration and the spotting patterns all vary dramatically from one specimen to the next. This particular fish actually took a dry fly in the early evening when terrestrials were being blown off the tundra into the river. Most char coming up for dries tend to be small fish under a pound and this one, three times that size, was a surprise. Perhaps because it had been in the river for some time it was feeling the pangs of hunger and decided to take a risk.

Sea-Run Cousins

Fishing for the sea-run char is an altogether different, more thrilling experience. Take the Greenlandic west coast rivers, for example—pulse after pulse of fish come up these rivers on each and every tide throughout the summer months. On many river mouths, admittedly, there are Inuit camps netting fish, but they are careful never to take too many, as they want their grandchildren to be enjoying this annual harvest in years to come. Sea-run char are generally much bigger fish, averaging 2 pounds or so and frequently topping 10, and they are magnificently colored—grilse-like silver when fresh from the sea and the most amazing crimsons and scarlets after some weeks in fresh water, the males being especially breathtaking. Like salmon, char fresh from the sea tend to be aggressive and still actively hunting, but once they've been in fresh water for any time they become more cautious, less quick to make mistakes and very difficult fish indeed.

Many of the Greenlandic rivers are crystal clear, and sight fishing is an important side of the game. You'll come upon numerous small groups, but keep walking these short, rapid rivers until you find the major areas of congregation. Sometimes there will be hundreds of fish spread over short areas of fast, rocky water. Some of these pools that I saw years ago I will never forget until my dying day. They simply take your breath away.

Grayling

I've fished for grayling in Canada, England, Scotland, Scandinavia, Europe, and Mongolia, and have no hesitation in saying they are my very favorite fish on the fly, for three good reasons. Number one, they are stunningly beautiful, with all manner of regional variations and a host of sub-species world wide. Number two, they tend to inhabit equally beautiful rivers. Number three, they're extremely canny and difficult to catch once they reach any size, so if you contact a good one you can feel genuinely proud of yourself.

One particular beauty of grayling fishing is that they can be caught in the coldest of weather, even when

---

CHAR-FISHING TIPS

Many weeks in Greenland have taught me certain important rules:

• Don't ignore foaming white water, because char will often hole up in the little pockets behind the rocks.

• Be prepared to change your flies frequently until you find the right pattern. I've had char on nymphs, lure patterns, and dry flies. Perhaps my favorite of all would be a moderately heavy, red-colored lure about 1–1½ inches in length, which might suggest shrimp. Black patterns work well, too, and I've caught fish on fluorescent greens.

• There are times when the fish will take absolutely everything, but when they're shy it pays to fish them cautiously, approaching on your knees. Make a couple of casts, and if you don't catch a fish leave the shoal for an hour or so before trying again. They really are that twitchy.

• These fish fight as hard as any you'll come across on fly gear, so don't be tempted to go too light. Even for 3- and 4-pounders, I'd say a 6- or 8-pound leader is about the minimum.

• With cautious fish you'll find they won't alter their position in the water a great deal, and that means you've got to place a fly pretty well on the char's nose. Sometimes a strike indicator can be used as a float to obtain and maintain exactly the right depth.

• The period around midnight, when the sun is at its lowest, is often the prime time for the wariest of fish.

• Congregations of the very biggest fish are frequently found right at the head of the river, so be prepared to strike out from base camp. Another advantage is that many other anglers won't bother with the trek!

• Think very carefully about your clothing. Walking and wading is almost essential, and that means Gore-Tex chesties. Be prepared for cold snaps, too, when the temperature can drop to uncomfortable levels for long periods, and take plenty of fleeces. Midges, mosquitoes, and evil, black, biting flies often proliferate. Nets, helmets, and creams are essential if you're not to go stark, raving mad. Don't forget high-factor sun cream for noses, lips, and tips of ears. Polarizing lenses are essential.

• At times, it might seem as though the river is alive with char, but this is deceptive. These are short rivers and you are possibly seeing the entire stock. The Inuit are conservative in what they take away, and they don't like sport fishermen staggering away with bags of dead fish. If you need a char to eat, fine, but put the rest back immediately. Unhook them in the water if you can. These are very wild, easily stressed fish, so treat them with great care.

there's cat-ice on the river margins, because even then they will still, at times, come up for a dry fly. However, most of my own grayling fishing is done on nymphs. All manner of nymphs will take grayling, but don't be fooled— the difficulty is to come.

By and large, they won't chase a nymph and they like to take it on a dead drift. So far so good, but now comes the real sucker-punch. You'll very rarely, even in crystal-clear

❧ WINTER GLORY

Grayling and winter are synonymous, and there's something about a heavy, smoking frost that really makes the grayling angler's heart beat fast. Mind you, they're not easy. The water will be cold and clear and the fish spooky. It's good to get as close to the fish as you possibly can so that you can watch their reaction to the fly and pick up on the very shyest of takes.

water, actually see a grayling take the nymph. I don't know why, but their body language is much more subtle than that of a trout. That's bad, but still worse is their ability to sip in and blow out a nymph in a millisecond. It happens faster than you can blink. They are probably the quickest fish on earth. You can fish a whole morning, have a hundred takes, and not touch a single grayling. It's as simple as that.

So what do you do? Well, like them or loathe them, a strike indicator of some sort is just about essential—that tiny red or yellow "float" that drifts downstream and registers your grayling take will boost your chances 20-fold at least. Lift your rod tip whenever the strike indicator does anything untoward— stops, moves sideways, moves upstream, zips downstream, or

goes under. Sometimes the fly will have caught bottom, of course, or snagged a piece of weed, but no matter. Strike at everything.

Always travel light and keep mobile when you are grayling fishing. Wherever the water, you'll tend to find groups of fish scattered here and there along miles of river. If you burden yourself with clothing and tackle you'll be reluctant to keep moving, and that's the key to finding fish and enjoying the best of the sport.

If you can, wade—you see how useful those Gore-Tex chest waders are proving to be? You thought they were an extravagant investment, but now you wouldn't be without them. The point is that your chest waders can get you really close to the fish, and that's what you need when you are grayling fishing. They bite so

quickly that you're simply going to miss them if you've got to cast long. Keep everything neat and tight and close up, and your catches will rocket. In fact, the Czech nymph technique that we discussed earlier was developed with grayling, more than trout, in mind.

In fact, Czech nymphing is the archetypal method for grayling, the perfect way of presenting flies neatly, precisely, and tightly to fish that don't give extravagant, slashing takes. Grayling are the obvious example, but there are several freshwater species, such as bream, that also respond well to this tactic. Don't scoff—the fight of a bream on fly tackle is something you are unlikely to forget.

⋏ A TORPEDO

Grayling are the most beautiful of fish, and it's a great shame that they're not more widely recognized worldwide for their cunning, their fighting abilities, and their handsome looks. Whether taken in North America, Europe, or Asia, grayling offer a supreme challenge. This fish was taken from Derbyshire, England. The biggest fish are perhaps in Austria or above the Arctic Circle. The most beautiful grayling are possibly the Asian strain found in parts of Mongolia and Siberia.

SALTWATER TIPS

• Never risk your safety when fishing the coast. Be quite sure you know when the tide is going to turn and have your exit route mapped out. Don't stay too long, however tempting the action may be.

• Don't venture out if the weather is due to change, and if you use a boat, make sure it's in tiptop condition, that you're wearing lifejackets, and that all your safety devices are up to scratch.

• Clean your fly line after each and every use to preserve it.

• Ensure that your reel is corrosion-resistant, or the salt water will wreck it in no time at all.

• Ensure that the flies you use in the sea don't mingle with your usual freshwater stocks.

• The seas and oceans are big places, but don't make the mistake of thinking that fish stocks are limitless. Occasionally take a fish that you and your family are going to eat at the end of the day, but return all others.

➢ THE PULSE OF THE RIVER

Stillwaters certainly have their charm and present a whole raft of challenges, but most anglers would probably agree that it is river fishing that really gets the adrenaline flowing. Water like this is magical—it's swift but shallow, and it's possible to sight fish and pick them off from behind rocks or in little depressions in the riverbed. In this particular case, in Siberia, we were fishing for survival. The trout and grayling were small, but without them the camp would simply have starved before the helicopter came to retrieve us.

Bait Fish

By bait fish, I mean many of the species that have been previously targeted by bait fishermen. Since the development of Czech nymphing, I truly believe that catching fish such as carp on fly will be the next major development in our sport. The surface is already being scratched, but there will be huge developments over the next decade or so.

Carp can often be caught on large imitations twitched in the surface film at the end of a hot day. Look for shallow bays where they are cruising and slurping in dead insects. Try a drowned crane fly or mayfly imitation. Jiggle it as a fish approaches, to send out a few enticing tremors.

Also, use the Czech nymph technique in water that's no more than 6 feet deep and is preferably shallow and clear enough to see the fish themselves. Try either Goldhead nymphs or, if these disturb the fish,

large black and brown nymphs. Allow them to trundle slowly downstream, and watch for very quick, easy-to-miss takes.

For chub, try any imitative dry-fly patterns or small fish-mimicking lures pulled back quickly.

⋏ THE NYMPH DOES IT
Really precise casting was necessary to trick this fish. The water was clear, the light was good, and you could see the fish move toward the large nymph as it twitched close to the bottom.

⋎ IN THE SURFACE FILM
This carp fell for a large fly fished in the surface film, where it was grubbing for fallen insects. The take was very definite but undramatic. The mouth opened, the fly disappeared, and the leader gave nothing more than a twitch.

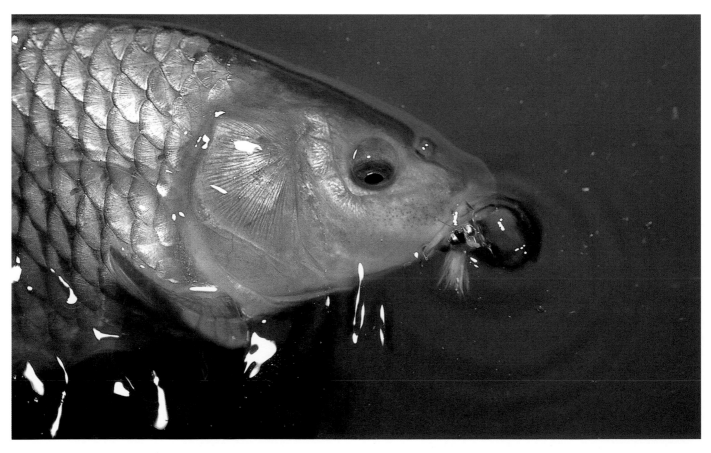

The World Is Your Oyster

With a range of fly gear and a large enough fly box you can tackle almost anything that swims in the waters of the world. As I've already said, there is already sharking on fly, and in India more and more anglers are targeting mahseer with fur and feather! How about the tiger fish in Africa? The barramundi in Australia? Nile perch in Egypt? Muskies in North America? The exotic sea species—even blue-fin tuna? It surely won't be long before someone targets a 6,000-pound great white shark with a fly tied to imitate a fleeing seal pup! The world of fly fishing is truly opening up in front of us all.

⋏ POT OF GOLD
Niels, a brilliant Danish fly angler, took this member of the carp family from the waters of the Ural delta on a tiny imitation. The crystal-clear lagoons were perfect for the fish.

◄ CHALLENGES TO COME
This shot is, to me, what fishing is, and can be, all about. You begin on your local lakes and rivers and you gradually progress to more distant venues in your own country. Then, perhaps after decades, you find yourself in a position to follow your dreams. Here I am, just after dawn, on the borders of China, looking at a river that feeds into the Amur Basin. I know that a day of incredible promise lies ahead of me, a day that as a child I could only dream of. All fishing is fabulous, but some of it is truly painted with magic.

TOP WORLD DESTINATIONS

Mankind has, for at least a thousand years, moved fish stocks from one country to another. With the carp family, transportation was not difficult as these fish are especially hardy and have comparatively low oxygen demands. With salmonid species, however, success rates were considerably lower. In fact, it was not until the later 19th century that advances in refrigeration and, especially, engine-powered ships enabled eggs and fry to be transported with a relative degree of success around the globe. The advance of technology, harnessed with the confidence and vision of the 19th century, resulted in there being hardly a country in the world that doesn't have stocks of trout somewhere. There are exceptions, admittedly, but they are few and it is more than likely that wherever a fly fisherman might land there will be possibilities close by.

Air travel has shrunk the world, so take advantage of this and try to get to as many places as possible. There's no doubt about it, travel not only broadens the mind, but rubbing shoulders with fly fishers from other continents hugely increases one's experience and understanding. Travel with a fly rod is an enriching experience. What I would like to do, therefore, is to take you on a whistle-stop tour of the world, describing things I've seen and done, experiences I've heard about, and challenges I can't wait to meet head on.

The Americas

A fly fisher could spend several lifetimes fishing the Americas alone. The wondrous scope of species to be found is quite mind-boggling… the gigantic king salmon, the phenomenal steelhead, and when it comes to trout, those of North America are as diverse as the States they dwell in. Their range extends from the Arctic Circle right down to the western coast of Mexico, and there are a staggering number of sub-species—Apache trout, Mexican trout, rainbows, red bands, golden trout, cutthroat, and the brown trout that were brought over from Europe in the 1880s. Then there are the char, generally a species of the deep, cold, clear waters of the north— Arctic char, brook trout, lake trout, Dolly Vardens, and more.

It's not just quantity, it's all about quality, too. The trout fishing in Montana is generally considered to be as good as it gets. I'd agree, but with the proviso that the wildernesses of British Columbia and Alaska take some beating. We haven't even mentioned the black bass fishing yet, or the bonefish of Florida, or the increasingly successful attempts to catch tarpon on the fly. Many of the American lure waters are also ideally suited to the fly fisherman, and how about the muskellunge on the fly— surely one of the greatest and wackiest challenges of them all.

Let's move south. How about the sea-trout fishing of the Falklands, Tierra del Fuego, and Argentina? The exquisite trout fishing along the Andes. Fly fishing for peacock bass in Bolivia perhaps! Or how about hunting out one of the most dramatic and unexplored fishing challenges of the century—the arapaima, resident of the Amazon and its tributaries. These mighty creatures, weighing up to 300 or 400 pounds, can be caught on spinners, so, if contacted, they'll surely take the fly.

What an amazing continent it is where you can take your fly gear from the frozen Arctic to the steamy jungles of Amazonia and catch a multitude of fish along the way.

Australasia

I have a friend, a traveling dentist, who has fly fished extensively throughout Australia, primarily for that giant, silver, estuarine perch, the barramundi. On occasion he has taken great delight in phoning me to describe his evening… perfect weather, deserted scenery, tidal rivers all to himself. Great bow waves in the margins and the barramundi coming in to feed. A hooped rod, a screaming reel, and a 40-pound thrust of silver bursting into the mellow air. And all this while I've been freezing at my desk in the UK.

Tasmania has wondrous trout fishing, but I have tended to fish in New Zealand, most specifically the South Island. Oh yes, I know that the North Island boasts Lake Taupo, but there's something about the wildness of the south that is uniquely inspiring. The beautiful Southern Alps offer some of the most thrilling lakes, rivers, and streams I have ever come across. Chillingly clear water, the remotest of locations, and the wildest of fish. On one trip to the South Island, the owner of the lodge I was staying at invited me to join the group in the helicopter to search out unfished waters. I declined politely, saying I'd fish the home river. He told me it was fished out, but I stuck to my guns and had the day of my dreams. Big browns, all on the dry fly and several near double figures in weight. The helicopter party returned and I told my host about my day. "There", he said, "I told you it would be useless!"

➤ NEW ZEALAND
The crystal rivers of New Zealand are well stocked with browns and rainbows, but they are often wild fish and can be very difficult to catch. There is a growing feeling that wild stocks need to be protected and that small streams in particular must be treated gently.

Asia

It pains me to say this, but think twice, thrice about going to Siberia and then, if you're sensible, turn the offer down. OK, perhaps it's willful to strike off such a vast territory, but my five journeys there have all been incredibly difficult, frequently dangerous, and virtually always unproductive. If it's mosquitoes you like, well then that's a different matter altogether.

But Asia is a massive place and there's still much to be done. It was in Kazakhstan, on the Ural River that forms the border between Europe and Asia, that I personally witnessed one of the greatest fly-fishing sights imaginable. Neils, a Danish fellow traveler decided to hunt out one of the massive Beluga sturgeon on his fly rod. It's several years now since the event, but I recollect that he broke a rod, lost two or three lines, and was smashed up in total perhaps six times. In the end, Neils hooked his sturgeon, took to his boat, and followed it for two grueling hours before finally

◁ HAPPY WITH HIS MOUSE
My Mongolian friend knows that the mighty taimen love to intercept mice as they migrate from one side of the river to the other. He's quite happy with my outlandish imitation.

maneuvering it into the shallow margins where he could beach it. You don't weigh fish that sort of size, but it's fair to say it was well over 250 pounds and Neils deserved every ounce!

I have a friend who's traveled extensively through the "Stans"— Tajikistan, Uzbekistan, Kyrgyzstan, and the rest—and he tells me the possibilities are enormous. For myself, my favorite country of all (how can I say such a thing?) is Mongolia. There I've fished a dozen rivers and found them all absorbing—magnificent scenery, an endless variety of fish, totally unspoilt waters, and some of the most welcoming people on Earth. I've been in a plane crash there, I've been stalked by bears, and I've been rendered almost paralyzed on the local vodka, but I'd go back again and again. Taimen are the lords of the Mongolian fly-fishing scene— an ancient landlocked salmonid species that science knows precious little about. They grow, perhaps, to 100 pounds, but you can expect them up to half that weight on a fly rod. And it is magnificent sport on swift, clear rivers hurtling through larch

➢ TOP BASS!
Bob James, the famous English angler, looks very happy with this excellent black bass. But it was quite a struggle. The fish was located in clear water about 8 feet deep. It followed several plastic lures right into the bank before turning away with disdain. Equally, a dozen fly patterns were also turned down. Eventually, a white, fluffy fly with no particular name was cast in and allowed to sink slowly. The bass came, looked, and as soon as the fly was twitched it sucked it in immediately. So, where there's a will there's a way!

forests with a backdrop of breath-taking snow-capped mountains.

And let's not forget India. Some of the trout fishing along the Himalayan ranges is staggeringly good. Possibly the most important three weeks of my entire life was spent in Kashmir. Perhaps it was the quivering, unworldly beauty of the place, with its subtle lights and endless landscapes of mountains, forests, and valleys. Perhaps it was the trout fishing, which was unbelievably good. Perhaps it was the knowledge that politics and soldiers and terror would soon snatch it from the fly-fishing arena that made it so precious and so special. To take a fly rod back to Kashmir is one of the ambitions of my life. There's trout fishing throughout India, however, especially in the hills away from the baking heat of the plains. And mahseer, the greatest of all the Indian species, can also be caught

on the fly. Yes, even if you remove Siberia from the equation, Asia still has a great deal to offer.

Europe

Good old Europe, a continent that isn't nearly as tired and as exploited as you might think. Ireland remains a jewel in the west and offers some of the finest wild brown trout and salmon fishing I, personally, have come across. Mayfly time on Lough Corrib is extraordinary, and if you're serious about your fly fishing then it's something that you just simply have to sample.

How about Scotland, especially the Western Isles? North Uist, for example, offers some of the most wonderful scenery combined with pulsating fishing for wild browns and glorious sea trout. Meanwhile, Wales is a maze of hidden valleys, and England still boasts its chalk streams, perhaps the cradle of fly-fishing civilization.

Scandinavian sea trout, char, and grayling are to marvel at. France has some impressive rivers. Surprisingly, so does Spain, and while General Franco did many things we would prefer to forget, he did at least stock the black bass that now offer endless exciting opportunities in this beautiful country.

Switzerland, the mountainous areas of Germany and Italy, and the

forested National Parks of Poland all have much to offer. The Czech Republic produces some of the best fly fishermen in the entire world and the rivers of both Bohemia and Slovakia are full of grayling and trout. To cap it all, the biggest grayling I've ever seen were in Austria. One summer morning, back in 1991, I nearly caught a 5-pound grayling, which came at the fly four times. Fate decreed he wasn't to be mine, but the memory still lingers. And let's not forget Slovenia—the rivers close to the town of Bled in the north are spell-binding.

My own, as yet unfulfilled, dream remains a visit to the Alta River in Norway. Friends have described it as Paradise—shallow and clear, with huge Atlantic salmon averaging 20 pounds or more coming to small flies on floating lines. You can fish at 3 o'clock in the morning, 10 o'clock at night, or whenever you wish. The valleys are garlanded in flowers,

there's no real darkness, and the great silver fish just keep on coming.

Africa

I make no excuses here. Africa is my blind spot, although I know from endless conversations that South Africa offers some wonderful sport on rivers such as the Sterksbruit, the Bell River, the Willow Stream, and the Witte.

Nile perch are now being taken on fly both in the river and on the lakes, especially Lake Nasser, where much research is being done by Englishmen like Charles Jardine.

I, personally, have flirted with Morocco and taken tiny trout there, but the Atlas Mountains retain their mystique. It remains a country of rumor and conflicting stories, but that's the fun of it all, isn't it? Strip all the mystery away and it would be much less of a world. There's just so much to see and discover.

> MONKEY BUSINESS
The salmon rod and reel are leaning against a tree, ready to do business with the mighty Indian mahseer, when along comes a monkey. When you're in camp, beware. These inquisitive creatures enjoy nothing more than a tour of your tent and an investigation of your belongings. If it's transportable, then they'll transport it and hang onto it until they get bored. Then, likely as not, they'll simply sling it in the river. That's certainly where I found everything from underpants to CDs!

GLOSSARY OF KNOTS

I T IS ESSENTIAL FOR EVERY ANGLER TO KNOW HOW TO TIE A SELECTION OF KNOTS. KNOTS ARE USED TO SECURE THE LINE TO THE REEL AND TO JOIN A HOOK OR LURE TO THE LINE. ALTHOUGH THERE ARE THOUSANDS OF DIFFERENT KNOTS, THE BASIC KNOTS ILLUSTRATED BELOW WILL BE SUFFICIENT FOR ANGLING PURPOSES.

HALF BLOOD KNOT

The half blood knot is commonly used for joining hook to line. This type of knot, when tied in nylon line, will not come undone.

⋏ STEP 1
Thread the free end of the line through the eye of the hook.

⋏ STEP 2
Pass the free end underneath the line and bring it back over the line to form a loop.

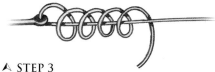

⋏ STEP 3
Continue to loop the free end over the line (as step 2) until you have approximately four turns.

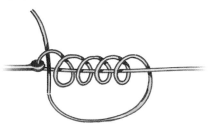

⋏ STEP 4
Pass the loose end between the eye of the hook and the first loop.

⋏ STEP 5
Pull on the loose end to tighten the knot. Trim off the end.

DOUBLE OVERHAND LOOP

Also known as the surgeon's loop, this knot can be used to create a loop at the end of a fly line, to which a looped leader can be attached.

⋏ STEP 1
To begin, double the end of the line back against itself.

⋏ STEP 2
Next, tie an overhand knot in the doubled line.

⋏ STEP 3
The doubled end should then be tucked through the loop again.

⋏ STEP 4
To finish, pull the knot as tight as possible and trim off the end.

BLOOD BIGHT

This knot has similar properties to the double overhand loop. If the end of the knot is not trimmed, several loops can be created to attach, for example, mackerel flies.

⋏ STEP 1
Fold the end of the line back against itself (this is known as a bight).

⋏ STEP 2
Cross the the doubled end once round the line.

⋏ STEP 3
Pass the looped end of the line back through the turn.

⋏ STEP 4
Pull the knot tight. Trim off the end of the line to finish.

WATER KNOT

This knot is also known as the surgeon's knot. The water knot is used to join two lines together, for example attaching a lighter hook length to the main line. The bulk of the knot will stop a sliding bead and can be useful when ledgering.

▲ STEP 1

Put the ends of the two lines alongside each other so that they overlap by about 6 inches.

▲ STEP 2

Take hold of the two lines and make a wide loop.

▲ STEP 3

Pass the ends of the line through the loop four times. Be sure to hold the two lines together.

▲ STEP 4

Pull the lines tightly so that the loop makes a knot. Trim the two ends.

BLOOD KNOT

The blood knot is also used to join two lines together. As in the water knot, begin by overlapping the ends of the two lines.

▲ STEP 1

Take one end and twist it four times round the other line. Then pass it between the two lines.

▲ STEP 2

Repeat with the other free end. Make sure that the first stage does not come undone.

▲ STEP 3

Wet the knot to lubricate it, then pull it tight. Trim off the two ends.

NEEDLE KNOT

The needle knot shown here can be used to tie solid monofilament to a fly line.

▲ STEP 1

Push a needle through the end of the fly line, Heat the needle until the line begins to bend.

▲ STEP 2

When cool, remove needle. Thread the mono through the fly line and five times round it. Bring the end back and hold it against the line.

▲ STEP 3

Now take the large loop and bring it several times round the fly line, trapping the mono.

▲ STEP 4

Pull on alternate ends of the mono to tighten. When the knot is firm, pull the mono tight.

A BRAID LOOP

Although some fly lines are fitted with braided lines for attaching a leader, it is a simple task to form your own from braided mono.

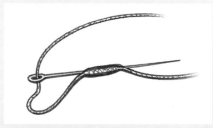

▲ STEP 1

Push a large-eyed needle into the braid. Thread the braid through the eye.

▲ STEP 2

Push the needle through the braid until the loose end emerges. A matchstick will keep the loop from closing.

▲ STEP 3

Adjust the loop until it is the size you require. Cut the loose end until it lies flush, and seal using waterproof superglue.

INDEX

Page references in *italics* indicate illustrations.

ACKNOWLEDGMENTS

AS EVER, PLEASE LET ME THANK JOHNNY JENSEN FROM COPENHAGEN AND MARTIN H. SMITH FROM NORFOLK, TO WHOM I KNOW I OWE SO MUCH IN TERMS OF FRIENDSHIP AND PHOTOGRAPHIC FISHING, HELP, ENCOURAGEMENT, AND ADVICE. WITHOUT YOUR SUPPORT, GUYS, I'D BE EVEN MORE FEEBLE BEHIND THE CAMERA THAN I AM NOW!

I COUNT MYSELF HUGELY FORTUNATE THAT I NOW SEEM TO HAVE A RAFT OF FISHING FRIENDS AROUND THE WORLD. IT'S ALMOST INVIDIOUS TO PICK OUT ANY OF THEM FOR FEAR OF OFFENDING THOSE LEFT OUT. THERE ARE HUNDREDS OF MEN AND WOMEN OF ALL RACES AND COLORS WHO HAVE HELPED ME WITH IDEAS ALONG THE WAY. IT WOULD, HOWEVER, BE WRONG NOT TO PICK OUT ROB OLSEN, THE ILLUSTRATOR OF THIS BOOK AND TRULY ONE OF THE BEST FIVE ANGLERS I HAVE EVER ENCOUNTERED. HIS SKILL IS ONLY MATCHED BY HIS SENSITIVITY. HAVING MENTIONED ROB, PERHAPS I CAN ALSO THROW OUT SUCH NAMES AS PHIL, ALAN, JOHN, PETER SMITH AND PETER STAGGS, MICK, LEO, AND IAN, AS WELL AS BOTH SAAD AND ANTHONY CRUZ WHO MAKE MY INDIAN EXPEDITIONS THE JOY THAT THEY HAVE BECOME.

FOR THIS BOOK IN PARTICULAR I MUST THANK PHILIP PARKINSON — ALWAYS A TRUE MENTOR; ALL AT SPORTFISH, ESPECIALLY DANNY NORTH AND JOHN WOLSTENHOLME; MY VERY OLD FRIEND DON ARLETT; ROBIN ARMSTRONG FOR ALL HIS HELP OVER THE YEARS; STEVE THORNTON; RICHIE JOHNSTON; LESLEY CRAWFORD; AND ABOVE ALL MICHAEL EVANS FOR HIS UNSTINTING AND UNSELFISH ADVICE.

I'D LIKE TO THANK JO HEMMINGS FOR HER CONTINUED SUPPORT THROUGHOUT THE YEARS, ANDREW EASTON AND KATE MICHELL FOR PERFORMING SO STERLINGLY AND, ABOVE ALL, CAROL SELWYN, WITHOUT WHOM NOT A SINGLE WORD OF THIS BOOK WOULD EVER HAVE APPEARED.